My Extraordinary Life

My Extraordinary Life

Alfred Wynne

authorHOUSE®

AuthorHouse™
1663 Liberty Drive
Bloomington, IN 47403
www.authorhouse.com
Phone: 1-800-839-8640

Published by AuthorHouse   04/15/2013

ISBN: 978-1-4817-9136-6 (sc)
ISBN: 978-1-4817-9137-3 (hc)
ISBN: 978-1-4817-9138-0 (e)

I dedicate my first book,

To Dawn Deon &Danielle.
For their everlasting friendship

Alfred.

I think that the place to start this my story is at the very beginning with my great grandfather, who lived in Whitford Flintshire on the Mostyn Estate. I don't know for sure but we could have a "Prince or rather Owen Gwynedd for our ancestor and therefore somehow related to the Wynnstay or the Gwydir Wynne's of North Wales. My great grandfather had many children one of which one turned out to be my grandfather Alfred, of who I am named after. My grandfather had three sons namely Arthur, Alfred and my Father Frederick who was left without his inheritance Robbed of it by his two older brothers as my father will explain in his following short account.

Over Twenty Years In Hell

I have of-times been asked to write the story of my varied life. Now at the apparently young age of thirty-six years, I find, if I am going to oblige my friends with my story I had better begin at once for my health is rapidly breaking down. I was born of humble parents in the year of 1900; my home to be was in the Edge Hill district of Liverpool. My father was a Clerk employed by a local firm of Cotton Brokers. A Welshman by birth and the wisest "man I never knew. Ambition was written all over him and in the Thirteen Years that I was blessed with his parenthood, I never knew him to have an enemy and during those few years, I watched a clever self-educated man climb the ladder of success in no uncertain manner. He believed just like the girl picking strawberries, in sticking to his bush and served with the same firm for many yeas, and in the year 1913 on my thirteenth birthday, he died and left a situation known in the profession as "Ring Salesman" he was Chairman and one of the founders of The Cotton Salesman Guilt a very fine organisation. My Mother who was devoted to him, did not survive him long, for five months later, she died broken hearted leaving two sons.

My Brother, who was some five of six years my senior, was employed by another firm of Cotton Brokers, whilst I was employed in the office of The Cotton Association. About a week after my Mother's death, I learned that my brother and I were to live with an Aunt, a sister of my late Father. I was informed that according to my Parent Will, their cash and household affects were to be evenly divided between my Brother and myself but, there was a clause which meant that we did not receive anything until we had obtained our "majority". That meant that my Brother would receive his share some five years before me. This was the beginning of my twenty years battle against fate and fortune. As I have said above, I was working in an office THE largest office of the Association and it is common knowledge that in an office, appearance is No: 1. Good brain and

1

good manners are naturally expected there. My wages of 5/-per week were eagerly snapped up by my Aunt. Naturally, I could not expect her to feed me for nothing, but what I did expect was that my Brother would at least provide me with suitable clothes if only to keep up my dear Father's good name. But, my expectations were shattered for when I appealed to my brother for assistance in this respect I found that he had developed a sudden hatred towards me and you may imagine my surprise when he told me if I wanted new clothes I should go out into the world and work and keep myself. I went upstairs to my bedroom with something like the Rock of Gibraltar in my throat, I could not realise the sudden change the world had taken. Yes! I cried and cried until I must have fallen asleep. The following morning my Aunt who usually called me to go to work, was surprised to find me already up and washed ready to go out, I was holding a cold sponge to my eyes to try and take away the inflammation, caused by my two or three hours crying. You are up early was my Aunt's first remark. Yes I answered my office hours seem to have ended. I will not be home to-night Aunt and give my love to the girls—meaning her two daughters whose ages where similar to my brother's.

What has happened have you lost your job Fred No, I am not going to the office any more, for as much as I like the work, it is not fitting in with you and A . . . My wages are too small to be wholly dependent on. Good morning to you Aunt.

Well, Liverpool is a big city surely there is some person who will find shelter for a willing boy. So, to town fist to seek a job where I am not known and my shabby suit would be more in contrast with the work. Walking up one street and down another, I suddenly came across a group of boys outside The Liverpool Education Committees Offices and on enquiring, I soon found that they were seeking work but they were more light-hearted than I was. I spoke to one boy and he advised me to go inside and get my name put on the waiting list—You will stand a better chance, he said, if you have your School Reference. My luck was in I had it in my pocket and quite a good one it was.

So, inside I went. Do you know of a vacancy for a boy? I enquired. Fill this form in and hand it back to me said a voice—here is a pen do you best writing, and spell correctly. Yes sir, I replied and began to do the necessary . . . Name Frederick . . . . Wynne . . . . Address? Oh dear! Come along sonny don't you know where you live? said a kindly male voice. Well sir, it is rather an awkward question to answer, you see, I left home this morning. Tell me young man he said, exactly what you mean. Well sir, I began, and I poured out my sad story, I did not mind who heard me it had to come out for it was choking me and after all, I had not committed a crime and was not ashamed. So that's it. Eh? I understand your feelings my boy, this kind gentleman said. Will you go a message for me, I want some tobacco? Yes sir, on my return from my errand he gave me a sixpence. I have often thought since, did he want that tobacco or was he afraid of hurting pride to give me sixpence without me earning it? Now then F . . . My boy, I have a great idea, you will succeed without the help of your Brother. How would you like to work in a Hotel where you could live in and so solve your problem of residence? Oh I would like that sir, very much I replied. Then take this letter to The Manager Adelphi . . . Hotel, and see what he can do for you. Thank you sir, and away I went with that precious letter in my breast pocket. On arriving at the Hotel, I approached a tall man with a smart uniform and the words 'hall porter' on the lapels. Can you direct me to the Manager's sir? I asked. I think he could see through my pocket and read the letter for he seemed knows right away the object of my errand. Hand your letter in at the office and sit down for a while my boy. Thank you sir and I carried out the instruction to perfection. While I was sitting I noticed two page-boys standing near and overheard one say—I have made half a dollar this morning how are you fixed? Four and a tanner was the quick reply and I want some more yet, it is my half day off.

My heart stopped beating to think that there was money to be made so quickly just then the Hall Porter beckoned me to an office with one word on the door 'MANAGER. Go inside Mr I . . . Is waiting to see you he said. Good morning young man are you the boy who brought this letter? Yes sir, I promptly replied. Well then he said, we have a vacancy here for a page-boy but you must qualify by examination in your own hand writing, here is the form of examination you can you sit here and fill it in, take your own time and when you have finished you can leave it on my desk and call and see me 9.0 am sharp in the morning. Yes sir, and I proceeded to read one of the stiffest list of questions imaginable, but my office experience no doubt helped me and roughly three quarters of an hour,

I was back in the street walking through a side street by the Market I noticed a workmen's dining rooms with a copy of the 'Menu' and price list chalked upon a black-board outside. Large bowl of soup with bread (2d) I suddenly felt that I was badly in need of some packing and decided on the soup. There were quite a number of men enjoying their midday meal. Suddenly one of these men walked from his table over towards me, as I looked up I recognized him as a neighbour of my Aunt, I will call him Joe Mac. Hello Fred . . . what brings you here he said. Oh I dropped in to try this soup, I replied. Buy you are out of your way here F . . . aren't you? There is no Cotton here. Well I said, if you must know, I have quit!

I Believe

By Alfred Wynne

I couldn't believe what I was hearing my eldest sister Ada telling someone about something that had happened in the War years.

My mother, Catherine called Kate, had been widowed in 1939, because my father had TB. My elder brother, Frederick, was serving in the Scots Guards and I was away from home, in Rhyl, suffering from TB. My mother was living at home in Liverpool with Ada and my other two sisters, Vera and Freda. My mother's sister-in-law, Auntie Maggie, was also staying in the house as she often did because her husband was in North Africa with the army.

On this particular day my mother had been sleeping late. She came down the stairs and was greeted by Auntie Maggie, "My God, Katy, you look dreadful!"

Yes", answered my mother, "I'm not surprised. I had an awful dream. I dreamt my boy Frederick was drowning in a pond. I tried to save him but I just couldn't grasp his hand. My arm wasn't long enough. As he struggled he went further away into the middle of the pond. I couldn't reach him. Then I saw a policeman and I woke up."

"Well, Katie, don't worry. Your dream has been broken because here comes a policeman."

"Oh no!" cried my mother. But my auntie assured her that everything was fine because this policeman was my mother's brother calling in for his usual cup of tea.

So my mother sat down to enjoy her breakfast prepared by my auntie.

Then came a knock on the door. My m other opened the front door and there stood another policeman.

"Mrs. Wynne", the policeman said. "Yes", my mother replied "It's about my son Frederick, isn't it?"

5

"No, mam" was the policeman's answer. "This is about your other son, Alfred (myself), in Rhyl in North Wales. He is dangerously ill. We'll be taking you to his bedside, if you could get ready quickly."

I was in Rhyl because I had been diagnosed with TB at a young age and had had to spend quite a lot of time in the Cleaver TB Sanatorium in Heswall, Cheshire. That was where I had found myself on the 3rd of September 1939, the start of the Second World War.

I remember that all the nursing staff was rushing about in panic. They were trying to organize some transport to evacuate us to Rhyl in North Wales. There was a government order, I believe.

I was then placed in a coach with many more boys and girls from Liverpool. Our supervisor had all of us singing the Welsh anthem, "Land of my Fathers", as we crossed into Wales from England. We arrived on the Rhyl seafront, in front of what was to be our new home. But we could only watch as all the staff ran out of our new home, afraid of catching TB. I think the new place was called "The John Jones Miners' Convalescent Home". But we could only sit on the coach and wait and wonder what it would be like in our new home.

All our own nurses were sent for from Heswall. When they arrived, they soon got cracking and we were housed and fed and roomed. We had only been there a few days when we were split up and I finished up around the corner in "The Stoke on Trent Convalescent Home".

One day, while playing in the lovely grounds of the home I complained about pains in my stomach. I was put to bed and Matron sent for the doctor who said it was something I had eaten. The matron wasn't satisfied and sent for another doctor who also couldn't find anything wrong.

The Matron had a doctor friend whose surgery was in Harley Street in London, but who happened to be at home in Rhyl on a break. She called him and I remember this big man standing over me in bed. He pulled back my bedclothes, put his hand on my stomach, then lifted me in his arms, took me downstairs to his car and drove very fast to the Royal Alexandra Hospital on the seafront. He took me straight to the operating theatre in the lift, giving me injections as we went up.

I awoke to find my lovely mother's face looking lovingly down on me. My appendix had burst and I was a very lucky boy to be alive.

The connection with my mother's drowning dream came after I had grown up and my mother had died in 1941. The war was still on and I was in the army in a barracks in Bulford camp, near Stonehenge in Wiltshire. It was a lovely summer's day and my mates wanted me to go swimming with them in a large pond close to the camp. I told them I couldn't swim, but they said I could just wade and paddle. So they persuaded me to go along with them. It turned out to be the worst decision I ever made.

I've read and heard people talking about being drowned and their experience of what it was like. Well. Now I was about to experience it for myself.

It was a lovely sunny day and me paddling in some fresh cool water, watching all my mates swimming. Suddenly the bottom of the pool wasn't there any more. I splashed with my arms but quickly went down to the bottom. I splashed all the times I was going down and coming up again. It was awful. I was very frightened. I knew I would drown. As I splashed and came up briefly I saw two men coming towards me. I reached out in panic and grabbed them, but only succeeded in taking them down with me. They both forced me off them and they left me.

I seemed to accept my fate after I heard bells ringing and saw all my life, things I had done, in vivid pictures spinning around. But then came the most wonderful feeling. I was sitting on the bottom of the pond fingering a rusty tin can and I felt wonderful.

Then I heard voices like when you come out of an anaesthetic and had the feeling of someone sitting on me as I lay face down on the bank. I heard someone say, "What regiment is he with?" I suddenly realized that I had been pulled out of the pond and was being resuscitated. I opened my eyes to see a half circle of feet and shoes in front of me. Lying there, I gathered my senses and then stood up and walked through the people with a word. I went straight back to my barrack room and picked up the book I had been reading before my mates took me out. I had no idea how I had been saved.

Then years later I heard Ada's story about my mother's dream and how in her dream she couldn't save my drowning brother. It seemed to me that later on, because she had passed over, she was able to save me. That is what I honestly believe, that my mother reached out and saved her son, me, Alfred, not Frederick, my brother from her dream. I was never afraid of water again, and I did learn to swim much later, and came near to being in the navy, which had always been my dream.

My Navy

I think the time must have been in the 1930s. I was a small boy in a sailor suit, holding my mother's hand at our front door, opened as we had a caller, a quite regular caller, a Gipsy lady with her sprigs of lavender.

"Lavender, lady?" the Gipsy said, "and I'll tell your future, and what about our little sailor boy?"

"Yes", my mother said, "he wants to join the navy when he grows up."

"Oh no", said the gipsy lady, "I'm afraid he will be in the army not the navy."

Anyway, with tears in my eyes we closed the door, my mother clutching her lavender.

We hadn't been living in our new house for long, moving from the centre of Liverpool to a new estate called Norris Green. The family was my mother, elder brother and sister, myself and younger sister, Vera. Freda come later and my father, well he was away at sea. We didn't see him very often apart from when he came home after his ship, the Duchess of York, had docked after her trip from New York, USA.

He would bring lots of presents. He even brought a cabinet gramophone on his back once, and another time four boxing gloves from a fight in New York's Madison Square Gardens, a famous boxing venue. The gloves had been raffled after the right and he had won the raffle.

While he was home one time he took me to see King George the Fifth and Queen Mary open the Mersey Tunnel. Afterwards, they opened the new East Lancashire Road. Then, one day, he came home discharged with TB after serving with the Cunard White Star. He soon became very ill, after he had organised his new method of making money for the family. We all of us, children as well, chopped and bundled firewood and made a living out of my Dad's effort. But then he had to go into Walton Hospital with his TB. He was only in two days, and he died.

My elder brother got a job making tea for the bricklayers building the Royal Court Theatre in Liverpool. My elder sister helped in the house, as did we all. With the help of the U.A.B., whatever that was, we were given coupons for everything my mother required to keep us alive, clothes and food. I remember how people looked down on us as we whispered to the shopkeepers and handed in our coupons for a pair of boots or a bar of soap.

Then came the time when my mother was struggling with my TB, trips to the doctor and to the TB Sanatorium in Heswall. My father had paid into an orphanage scheme while he was in the Merchant Navy. So my mother thought about thinning her family by putting her children in Homes.

I remember my mother taking my younger sister, Vera, and myself to the Seaman's Orphanage in Newsam Park, Liverpool. When we got in through the gates I saw all the boys marching in their sailor suits and some more boys climbing the rigging mast. I was in my element, I wanted to stay. This was my navy at last. But it was not to be. They were prepared to take me, but not my sister. My mother said, "Both or none". But it was only for boys. So the Gipsy long ago could be right. Anyway, I was soon back in the TB Sanatorium from where I was evacuated in Rhyl in North Wales when the Second World War broke out. After some time I left there and my mother brought me home to the Liverpool blitz.

I was working in the Adelphi hotel. One night, in an air raid, I was waiting for my 14 tram to take me home when a landmine (a large bomb on a large parachute) hit the Walker Art Gallery. I was standing in Lime Street opposite the public house, the Legs of Man, next to the Empire Theatre. I was blown into the pub and came round behind the counter without a scratch.

My poor mother was taken ill with pleurisy and pneumonia, made worse by taking her in and out of the Anderson shelter. She died at home but with me at her bedside with a priest. It pleased me in later life to think I was there with her, my lovely mother. Then my elder sister and her boyfriend were left to bring us up. But while she was bringing me up her boyfriend was in charge and he laid down the law with a firm fist. He locked the larder door so I couldn't get more food for me and my sisters. I was his worst enemy. As young as I was, I did all kinds of things to make him mad. In the end, I ran away to my grandmother in Old Swan, Liverpool.

She had my mother's brother's family sleeping upstairs and she sent me up. It was very late. They put me in bed with a young boy, my cousin. There were babies' nappies drying in front of the fire, drying but without being washed. The smell was awful. As I lay there was a rustling g sound and a lot of squealing noise. I lit a candle and what I saw was a roomful of rats. I got dressed and ran out into the streets again.

I went towards Brunswick Road where I believe I was born. At the end of Brunswick Road was Shaw Street where all the doss houses were, a bed for the night for a shilling. In the doss house I met another lad who said he was going to sea. I said, "What do you mean/" He explained he was going to get a job working on the ships while they were in dock. It was my chance to find my navy, so I did the same as him, but not on his ship. I worked in the galley as we sailed off to America. I was talking to a steward on the ship and he said all I could do was see America from the ship. I must not disembark. So that was my navy, I thought.

When I got back home I got an anchor tattooed on my arm. My elder sister went mad and said my elder brother would be coming to see me soon to get me away from her and her husband as she was struggling with a family as well as me and our younger sister, Freda. My elder brother, Fred, had married a girl in Kingston-on-Thames, while he was serving in the army. My brother's in-laws decided I should go to live with them in Kingston, Surrey.

So with a few instructions on how to get there, I left my job at the Adelphi, which I had gone back to and set off from Lime Street Station for Euston with a little suitcase. From Euston I got the tube to Waterloo Station and a train on from there to Norbiton, near Kingston-on-Thames. By the time I got there it was 11.30 pm and there was laughing and singing as I was led from the street door into the living room. There were my relations, a soldier and a sailor, with my brother's wife, her two sisters and their mother, all very happy in spite of the bombing going on.

Before I could put my suitcase down my brother's mother-in-law said to me that the Labour Exchange would be open at 9 a.m. for me to get a job. Well, that's exactly what I did. The very next morning I was offered a job in the Kingston Hotel because I had worked in the Adelphi. But this times the job I was offered was as a waiter. As I hadn't been to school, I dreaded the job and my first and last problem was to come after a couple of weeks. An awkward customer said I had charged him too much—my worst fear! Anyway, I asked the headwaiter to check it for me and he said, "You're right; he's wrong". So I took his change back to him and he went mad, calling me in obscene language a thief. Well, I'm afraid I lost it and saw red. I picked his plate up and hit him in the face with it. Well, that was that.

So I walked around Kingston and found garage advertising for staff to make sten guns. I applied and got a new job before I had to tell my brother's mother-in-law I had been sacked. I soon came off making sten guns to do more mechanics's work, and was accepted by most of the staff.

One day, one of the mechanics asked me if I would like to go out to deliver a car. The car was a beautiful Bentley. We went out to Coomb Woods and to my amazement we drove past two American GIs on duty. We were stopped for our identity to be checked. My driver produced the necessary documents and we drove in towards this beautiful house. When we got back, he told me that that was where General Eisenhower stayed. To go out in these cars was out of this world. We took an S.S. Jaguar to someone else.

I thought it was now time for me to join the Navy, so with time off from work I took a train to Portsmouth, with several other young lads with the same idea. But the train was involved with enemy action and stopped for a while. When we got to Portsmouth Naval Recruiting Office I sat outside the room as some of the lads went in and out, looking very pleased and saying "Fleet Air Arm, Home Fleet" etc. Then it was my turn to enter the room. Two officers sat behind a big desk with the white ensign on the wall behind them.

"Well, lad, let's have your identity card."

I searched through all my pockets in vain. I didn't have it with me.

"Sorry, son", the officer said. "WE can't go any further without your identity card".

So the Navy wasn't for me. I wasn't going on that journey again. So I got off the train at Kingston and went round to the Army Recruiting Office. That Gipsy must have been right after all.

"So you want to join the Army, lad. When were you born?"

"12th of November 1927", I said, making myself two months older than I really was.

"What regiment do you require?"

"The Scots Guards", I said.

"Well, we'll give you a little test, an arithmetic test. No, son, you failed the test. What would be your second preference?"

The poster said, "Artillery". I pointed to it and he said "OK, son". After he took my address, he said, "We will be in touch, but first I want you to swear this oath. Raise your right hand and repeat after me—I swear to do my duty to God and to the King, etc".

A few weeks went by and then I got a letter and a railway warrant to report to the Artillery regiment at Winston Barracks in Lanarkshire, Scotland. I was to be there for eight weeks without going outside.

The first thing the sergeant said was, "You will make out your will to your next of kin". I made my mother my next of kin. The next thing was to draw out all our kit, including my rifle.

The course was very hard. The next thing was I lost all my hair thanks to the camp barber. Then we had to degrease our rifle and clean it, get our bedding from the quartermaster's store, make our beds, and go to the canteen for something to eat. After that, we had to pack up our civvy clothes to send home, then Blanco green all our webbing: big pack, small pack, and straps; two small pouches; belt and garters. Polish all the brass that goes with them. Then, when your kit was good enough for the company sergeant, you could go to bed.

The next morning about five o'clock I awoke to the sound of a Scottish piper standing at the foot of my bed in full Scottish dress. This was to be my morning reveille every morning for eight weeks. Welcome to the army, Mr. Wynne. So here it is in all its glory, the army: some days, physical training; some days, the rifle range; another day, throwing hand grenades; and all the time, spit and polish. What I did like, though, through all this was our route marches.

We would set off on a ten mile march away out of Lanark and towards "Mount Tinto". We would march with all our kit and our rifles, a very gruelling march. But about a mile from our barracks our Scots band would be waiting for us on our way back. The pipes and drums would start up and we would straighten our backs, take a deep breath and march like guardsmen, very proud, and our tired bodies would feel a lot better.

Then came the true reason we were being turned into supermen. We were issued with new kit: knife and fork and spoon and razor, all made of a material as light as a feather, and we were told we were to fight the Japs. Then we practiced doing just that. A section of the camp was made to look like a Far Eastern jungle and some of our own lads were dressed as Japanese soldiers. We had mock battles with them, with unarmed combat and explosives. We had to go into gas chambers with our gasmasks on, and after walking in a circle for a while we had to take our gasmasks off. The gas chamber was filled with tear gas. We were so pleased to get out of there!

Then when they said we had completed our eight weeks Basic Training, I passed out with flying colours. I had the best score in the rifle shooting. I had five rounds and put them all in the bull at the centre of the target. The sergeant asked if he could keep my target to show the next intake. We were told we could not go out, so a group of us lads, with our hair all grown back, went off to Glasgow, where we found a small café where you could put half a crown on the counter and eat your fill.

My next camp was Bulford, the camp near Stonehenge where I almost drowned. We continued our training. I was trained on 19 and 22 Radio sets and also on driving 15 cwt trucks and 3 ton Dodge vehicles. In the dance hall, we danced to the Glen Miller Orchestra. After training at Bulford we went to Watchet in Somerset, and enjoyed being in a nice small village but also being let loose on the town of Taunton and on cider. We were trained on twenty-five pounder field guns, which we fired on Exmoor. I then found myself in Rhyl again, in Kinmel Park Artillery camp, then the Royal Artillery camp in Larkhill near Stonehenge.

This was where I went to Amesbury one evening and found a local church social. I walked in through the door to find a tea bar with a beautiful young girl serving. She handed me a nice welcome, cup of tea and a lovely smile. I went into the main hall where they were dancing to a gramophone record. I sat myself down in a corner when the girl from the tea bar asked me to dance. I tried to tell her that I had just walked from Larkhill, and anyway was wearing my Army boots, but she would not let me off the hook. She insisted that we dance, and after a while we both sat down together. I think I fell in love with her. We made a date for the next day. We kissed goodnight and I started back on my long walk to the camp, only to find all the lights on. All my pals were packing their kit.

"What's going on?" I asked. They said, "We're moving out".

"When?"

"In an hour."

I thought, "What about my date?" I scribbled an apology to Christine and tried to find someone who wasn't leaving, but I found no-one. I often wonder how different my life might have been, but that's war for you.

Our next stop was the Royal Artillery Grand Headquarters Department at Woolwich in London. Woolwich was OK but very regimented with Redcaps (Military Police) everywhere. But I soon began to enjoy my new home. I could sit and listen to the Royal Artillery Band rehearsing in the grand Hall or go to the Woolwich Empire, My mates made me enter a singing competition by Carol Levis and I won. Then there was the Welling Embassy where we could dance and have a drink or two, just as happened one night when I was going back from the Embassy to our barracks. Just me and another gunner pal were walking and talking. Then ahead of us there were to Redcaps.

I had my cap tilted off my forehead and back a little. The two policemen followed us as we walked by. One of them shouted, "Hey, you!"

I said to my mate, "Keep walking".

Then one of the caught us up and swivelled me around. "Why didn't you stop?"

"I don't answer to 'Hey, you'. I have a rank, even if it is only gunner. You should have addressed me correctly, corporal", I said.

"Oh, we have a smart one here, don't we?" He then started to put my name, rank and serial number in his little book.

"I said, "That's a cushy good job you have there!"

Well, four policemen lifted me off my feet and I was put into the back of the 15 cwt truck that was nearby. I was handcuffed to the inside of the truck and driven off to the Woolwich guardroom. I was told to strip and the station sergeant and a corporal searched every inch of my clothing as I stood there completely naked, shivering with the cold. Then after about half an hour they threw me my trousers and vest, and three mattress sections which together would make one mattress. They took me to a prison cell with iron bars on the front, and locked me up for the night—with no cocoa (ha-ha). The next thing was the rattling of my prison bars as one of the policemen put his truncheon along them.

"Come on! Get up! Get out!"

I said, "What about my breakfast?"

"You've missed that. You were too late. You'll have lunch at midday, but for now . . . here." He handed me a mug of water and a slice of bread.

"Now, take that yard broom and that bucket and get scrubbing the cobblestone yard."

That was my day job from then on. With blisters on my hands I took the punishment.

After about a week I was told that my battery officer was coming to try to get me out of this punishment. My officer turned up to interrogate me about what I had done to land myself in prison. The lad who was with me when I was picked up was asked questions as well. My offence was "not wearing headdress", which wasn't true. My friend told the truth. The police were wrong, he said. I had been wearing headdress but it was pushed back on my head.

"Ah", said my officer, "this is false arrest. We've got them. You won't be here much longer".

Then they released me, they said, because I was being sent on embarkation leave. That is what happened when I got back to the barracks. Free and going home! That felt good. My embarkation leave soon finished and I had to report to the transit camp at Huyton, Liverpool, where my unit was directed after their leave. We assembled on the landing stage, with the troopship towering over us.

We set sail for somewhere in the Far East (that's all anyone knew). We passed Gibraltar, Malta and on to Port Said, Egypt, where we stayed a while and then through the Suez Canal to Aden. As we proceeded, news came about the Hiroshima atom bomb. We were told about the surrender by the Japs. This news was welcomed by all, but we had already turned and were sailing back.

The next destination was Salerno in Italy where, after a few days off the troopship, we began to make our way towards Rome and eventually Milan. We went the length of Italy, through Trieste, and into Yugoslavia, where I finally rejoined my regiment, the Second Medium Regiment Royal Artillery. They were resting after they had fought in the Italian campaign. We slept under canvas, in a bell tent.

The first morning on parade the Commanding Officer came on parade in dressing gown and slippers, as did some other senior officers. No one seemed to care. "Find them something to do, Sergeant Major, and fall them out."

"Battery, dismiss!" came the order, and we fell out to our different jobs. This was more like it! The sun shone, the officers were nowhere to be seen, and the NCOs couldn't care less. We had lunch in the open and you could tell which onions on your plate were and which were wasps' wings. After lunch, we were told why we were there, that is, in Trieste. It was our job in Trieste to keep the peace. The Fascist Italians were at war with the Communist Italians. We were told to hand in our rifles and we were issued with Thompson sub-machine (known as Tommy guns). I thought I had joined the Cosa Nostra or the Mafia!

Trieste, when we got down to it by a winding mountain road which went down for miles, was worth it. There was no sign of war here now, and the shops were full of food. The lovely restaurants were full and the tramcars were running. One day, I was on a tram when it stopped because a woman with a Scouse accent wanted to get off. For a minute, I thought I was in Lime Street! I got off as well, caught up with her and asked whether she came from Liverpool. She invited me to her home. We turned a corner and she stopped at a big ornate door.

"This it," she said, as the door opened and there stood her maid.

Well, it was a marble mansion inside. The walls, floor and ceiling were marvellous. If she had said it was Mussolini's house, I would have believed her. Over a nice cup of tea, she explained how she came to live in this palace. She said her husband had been a spy for the British, and as a thank you gift they gave him this house, and, of course, after the war ended she joined him. Later, I went to a restaurant and ordered spaghetti, or what they call Pasta Shuta. It was a huge helping, and that was the starter. Afterwards came my main meal of steak, eggs and chips. I had a Vino Rosso (the red wine) to wash it down. I was ready to take on all the Communists and Fascists by myself! I joined up with some of the lads and we went to where we heard some shots and people singing, "Avanti, popolo!" the Communist anthem.

It soon quietened down and we went back up the long winding mountain road. We stayed there for some months until we had settled the problems between the two warring groups. Then we moved to Treviso, in the Venice area. We occupied a barracks built by Mussolini, a fine square of beautiful buildings. We used to go out to Padua, Mestre, Venice, Milan and some other places. There was a skiing resort not far away by truck, a very famous one. We visited a very good hotel there and enjoyed being pampered. Our uniforms would be cleaned while we had a shave, a haircut and a shower. We would come out of all this and sit in the main bar with the gentry and officers of the American army, and the Blue Devils, an American military police unit.

Another time, I was sent to Mestre to look after British very hard military prisoners. They would come out of the cells, walk a few steps and then go into a circus round lions' cage for their exercise. As I walked beside one of them, a murderer, he said to me, "Just look the other way". I said, "If you make me, I will shoot you", and I pushed him into the cage. None of them tried it on again.

One day, I was posted to Venice to guard the HQ on the Grand Canal. I challenged an officer one night and asked him for his ID. To my surprise, it was Monty himself with his entourage. They came in a motor launch. Another time, I was out in St Mark's Square on a break, and got talking to some sailors from a destroyer off the Lido. We had a good time together until I found myself on the destroyer. I think it was the Phoebe, or something like that. Anyway, they brought me back to St Mark's in the Liberty boat. I love the Navy. A few days after that, we had to go to the Opera House in Padua where Monty addressed the garrison.

Then came an order for some of us to go home. They were holding Victory Parades in different cities. Mine was of course the city of Liverpool. We went back by train. We first came into beautiful

Austria. We camped in a German camp in Villack. This is where I got rid of my pistols. I was scared of being caught with them. I had an Army Webley revolver, an Italian Beretta automatic and a very nice German Luger in a polished wooden case which when attached to the Luger made it into a sort of small rifle. But I threw them away.

We went to Salzburg. It was beautiful in the moonlight with the snow capped mountains. It had me writing poetry. We travelled through all these countries by train, Italy, Austria, Germany, and France. We saw all the devastation the war had caused. Cologne Cathedral was black from the fires that had burnt around it. It was the same all the way to Calais where we took the ferry to Dover. We spent the night in Dover Castle.

We marched through the streets of Liverpool, finishing up in the Anglican Cathedral. There was an address by the Mayor and various dignitaries. After a few days' leave with my elder sister it was time to go back to the transit camp. Then it was Dover Castle and through France, Germany etc, back to Treviso, for some soldiering again.

Then one day I was approached by an officer who told me he had been selected as Entertainment Officer. He planned to put on a camp play called "Men in Shadow", and had thought of me for the part of the Commando soldier. I jumped at the chance. The play was by Mary Hayley Bell, John Mills' wife. After many rehearsals we put it on and it was a great success. We even took it to other units.

On another occasion, I accompanied Ivy Benson and her girls' band on their visit to the troops. I even took out one of her girls, Victoria England. Well, that's what she called herself. Then one day I had a welcome surprise. I had been selected to go on a cruise with the Royal Navy. "Ah, at last!" I thought, "My Navy day is here". I joined some others from different units and set sail for Malta. It seems this was to be a Fleet exercise.

When we got to Valetta harbour my eyes lit up. There in front of me was the whole Mediterranean fleet in the harbour and just outside. It was amazing to see so many capital ships. We were put ashore in barracks and allowed out on the town. Well, I've never seen so many sailors, and I joined them. They introduced me to all the naughty places. The most famous street in Malta, for all the wrong reasons, was Straight Street, known as The Gut. We saw Philip Mountbatten there and some lads from the Phoebe.

We stayed out all night, I think, because we finished up on the other side of the island. Navy trucks took us there, some Army pals and me, but we missed the last bus back to Valetta. "What will we do now, Scouse?" came the call for help to me. Well, we started walking and then I saw a bus in the front garden of a house. This was because the bus drivers then in Malta took the buses home.

It was dead easy to pinch the bus. Back in Valetta, we just left it outside a shop and walked back to our barracks. No one complained, so we were free to join the Fleet the next morning. A Liberty boat took us out to the ships. We are allotted. Imagine my surprise at being allotted to HMS Liverpool. No one wanted this except me because it was the flagship, with all the bull that went with it with the Admiral aboard. He was Lord Louis Mountbatten, and to all the Royal Marines aboard it looked like a daunting task to work on board. But I remembered what a sailor had told me the night before, "Get a job in the galley".

The time came for us to sail. The bugles sounded then the bosun's whistle, then the command, "Hands for leaving harbour". The grand salute came from Valetta HQ as we gracefully passed out from Malta and into the Mediterranean. We had been stood to attention on the deck during all this ceremonial departing. It sent shivers up my spine to be part of this event. All I'd ever dreamed of was coming true.

So we, HMS Liverpool and I, were soon well into the Med. I was working down in the galley as a veg chef. Then to bed on the first night in my Navy. I was wakened by the shouts of, "Come and see this!" I went up on the quarterdeck to get a better view. For there all around us were ships of all the allied navies from the war just fought, aircraft carriers, cruisers like mine, battleships, frigates, destroyers, submarines, depot ships: an assemblage never before seen and never likely to be seen ever again. It was a celebration for the end of the war and how privileged was little old me, late in the day, to be invited to all this.

We were told over the tannoy system that the exercise was about to begin, and mock battles would be fought by all the navies. I went back on deck, not to miss a thing. Then it started: gunfire, aircraft zooming everywhere firing their cannon, ships ablaze! We were told to light oil drum fires to make believe we had been hit. I was pushed into the sea like many others off a lower part of the ship as the tannoy announced, "Abandon ship!" We were playing big boys' games, but how exciting it was! I was truly in my Navy. This went on all day long. I think by the sound of the gunfire they were using up all the surplus ammunition from the war. I will never ever forget what I witnessed that day.

The next day, we anchored off Genoa in Rapallo Bay. It looked like a paradise and made a wonderful picture from the ship where I was standing in line to board the ship's Liberty boat to take me ashore. I had now passed my twenty-first birthday and was allowed to stay on shore all night. This was also because I was a veg chef and didn't have to do a duty watch. I was certainly enjoying life. The sailors were a great bunch, who addressed each other as "Horse", as I learned one day as I was lining up for my grog (tot of rum) one day aboard. Most of them were Scousers so I was well at home with them. Ashore, we met some Italian and French girls and had a great time. We got the first Liberty back to the ship the next morning. On that day we left to sail along the Italian coast, continuing along the French coast and the Riviera.

The first place we went ashore after Genoa was Bizeta, where I found that everyone in the town congregated in a huge square every evening, chatting to each other and walking up and down the square. What a good idea, I thought.

The next Liberty took us to Philipeville where, as the lights came on in the evening, we mingled with the soldiers of the Foreign Legion, who all seemed to be broke. I remember buying a drink or two and even giving some cash to a few of them. I felt sorry for them, as it wasn't at all like Beau Geste.

In one of the places we visited along the coast I was sitting in a café all alone with no-one to talk to. On the next table was a smartly dressed black man. He was alone also. He was very well built and about my age. He looked about the size of Paul Robeson. I went over and introduced myself to him, which is how I am, and to my surprise he spoke English better than I did. We discussed everything from political situations to the stars. He told me he was a headmaster at a school somewhere nearby. He offered to show me where he lived and I accepted. We went out of the café, or bistro, to his car and he drove me to his home. It was very nice where he lived. He was single and lived alone. He had some nice ornaments and paintings in his living room, and nice carpets. We sat together chatting some more over a very nice cup of tea and then he drove me back to the café where I waited for my other pals. I loved the experience of my black friend's knowledge of so much and I was happy to have met him.

Further down the coast, we, that is the ship's company, were invited to a vineyard. As we arrived there we were greeted by the owners and on a huge, lovely green lawn there was a long row of trestle tables lined up, with their snowy white tablecloths fluttering in a gentle breeze. All the decanters and glasses were glinting and there was seating for everyone. First, the owners wanted to show us around the inside of the building, with all the huge wine barrels and everything else that is needed for winemaking. It was very interesting and made me think back to my time working in the wine cellars at the Adelphi in Liverpool. Part of my job then was to fill a gentleman's decanter every night and he was the owner of three vineyards in France before the war, but was then a refugee in England. After our tour inside we came to the tables on the lawn to drink our fill of wine.

On we sailed along the coast to another interesting little town. I remember as I sat in a bistro with two Army pals that there was a bit of a fair outside, with a rifle range. The girl who ran the stall was very pretty, with dark hair. We went to the range and started shooting, trying to win a prize or make an impression on the girl. One of my pals said, "It's a fix. The sights have been tampered with". The girl heard him. She vaulted over to our side of the stall, loaded his rifle and promptly, Bang! Bang! Bang! Scored three bulls eyes. We slunk back to the bistro as if we had been shot. She was like Annie Oakley in the film "Annie Get Your Gun".

We were still sitting in the bistro when a young English lad parked his bicycle outside and came to our table. He said, "Nice to see English men". We asked, "Where have you come from?" "I've come from Surrey and I'm on my way to see my brother. He's in the Army in Tripoli".

He had a drink, got back on to his bike, and off he went. We then asked if we could play table tennis on the table. We wanted the nets and the bats and balls. We tried to ask in French with back-up sign language but the café-owner couldn't understand us. Then who should come in but "Annie Oakley", the girl from the rifle range. She said to the proprietor, "Ping pong". "Ah, ping pong!" We tried to hide our blushes as we thanked Annie.

The next place we stopped at was Monaco, where we really lived it up, then on to Gibraltar and swiftly back to Malta. You see, my dear mother was right to dress me in a sailor suit all those years ago, and the gipsy was—half-right!

In Malta, we quickly got back to normal. We left the ship, the HMS Liverpool, in Valetta and soon after returned to Treviso. But later, when we were packing again, and when we heard where we were off to, I just couldn't believe it. I knew there was a bit of a war going on in Palestine, but it wasn't that I was thinking about, it was the memory I had of my CO stopping me, back in Rhyl, from joining the Palestine police. Even more strange, they chose me to be one of the men forming the advance party to prepare the camp at Rafah in Palestine, for the rest of the regiment who would follow in the not too distant future.

We sailed from Trieste, called at Salonika in Greece to deposit our horses, stayed a while, then sailed on to Port Said in Egypt, a fascinating place, full of flies. We were to stay under canvas again, bell tents, and we suffered a few sandstorms. But we were allowed to go out to Ismailia, that is, if you were not chosen for guard duty. I went on the town with my mates, Hopper, Sharp and Best, a Scotsman. Hopper came from Newton-le-Willows; Sharp from Stoke, Best from Dunfermline, and, of course, yours truly from Liverpool. We were the Crazy Gang when we let loose together. The young Egyptian boys would pester you to let them give you a shoeshine. The blacking was liquid, so they would threaten to cover your nice clean pressed tropical uniform with it if you refused to let them polish your boots. And for a few piastre's it wasn't worth refusing them.

Then some other boys would offer their sisters for—you know what. And they tell me, because I was never tempted, that the sisters were little boys dressed as girls. There was a time when Best was tempted to sell his wristwatch. The money offered was very good. The Egyptian took us to the buyer, a merry dance through one street and then another, until he stopped at what seemed to be the front door of a house. He took the watch to show the buyer, and we waited and waited for him to come out. When we eventually opened the door, we found it was an alleyway to the next street. Poor Best never saw the man, or his watch, ever again. Everything there was trickery.

Eventually we found ourselves out of bounds and in a dangerous position. We were in this house full of prostitutes and huge Egyptian guards. A jeep full of military police came. Best, Sharp and Hopper were all taken by the police and booked for being out of bounds but I had hidden under a bed. I then found myself alone and in danger. The guard was blocking the door as I tried to escape. I bluffed him and threatened to kill him, and he moved out of my way. I dashed out into the street. I didn't know where I was but I hailed a gharry (a horse-drawn coach) and jumped behind the driver. I said, "I will kill you if you don't get me to the 'Blue Kettle'". We galloped all the way and I got back to our tent. There was no sign of the 'Three Musketeers', so I snuggled down to sleep. Then the three of them came into the tent, talking about the punishment they were going to get.

"You didn't get caught1"

"No," I said. "I had a lovely time. Sorry, lads, you'll have to excuse me. I'm very tired." I was killing myself laughing to myself under my bedclothes.

Well, all this fun couldn't last. One day, we were to board our train from Egypt to Palestine. It was a special for us only, a small group who made up the advance party, including myself, two officers, Major Black, a Scot and Captain Watt Davies, who was Welsh, a sergeant and six gunners, one of whom was our chief, if you could call him that. Our first stop was under Mount Sinai, where Moses received the Ten Commandments.

I rose early because I had been fed up with my lousy breakfasts, so I thought I would cook my own. I was enjoying this cooking, outside the train, when Major Black showed up in his dressing gown.

"That smells good," he said. Could you do some for me and Captain Davies?"

"Yes, sir" I said. Then he said, "From now on you will be our cook."

"Thank you, sir." Off he went back to the train with his two breakfasts.

"That's good," I thought. "No more guard duty! I'm the new chef."

We left the Sinai desert and proceeded to Gaza. We detrained there. Eventually we came to our new camp where the rest of us were to be stationed with our big guns in the Rafah sub-district. I was just wondering where was this war everyone was talking about when there was the sound of two explosions quite a way off, and then some sporadic gunfire which seemed not too far away at all. That was to be our occasional orchestra from now on, explosions and gunfire.

The regiment soon got organized. We even had time for a special person to come and lecture to us on the atom bomb and the way to stay safe from it. I think he was someone called Professor Rutherford, who had something to do with the making of the bombs dropped on Hiroshima and Nagasaki. He explained there was first the flash, then the bang, then the fallout. If you could shield your eyes and face and any bare skin, then hang on to something when the blast came like a hurricane, and then try to avoid the fallout, you would be Ok. So it was all useless info we were given.

That night we were told that our rifles and any other weapons would be chained to our wrists, and the only way the Jews would be able to take them away from us would be to cut off our hands. This they were known to have done. So, welcome to Palestine, lads! When it was my turn to stand guard, I had to climb the steps of a wooden lookout tower. My equipment consisted of a searchlight, a brass Verey light pistol and a Bren gun chained to my body. I sat up there freezing, because the heat of the day was complemented by the cold of the night, and it was cold. The night was jet black and everything you could see seemed to be moving the more you stared at it. Yet in the morning it was a large rock or something else that couldn't possibly move.

We had heard tales of Jews who had come from Blighty and that they were here in Palestine joining the terrorists. In one camp, they invaded, took the armourer captive and killed the Commanding Officer. There was another rumour about three sergeants being hung from a lamp post in Haifa. As well as on guard duty, when we went out and about in Palestine we had to have our rifles chained to our wrists. As we went along the roads, there were Jews holding money in their hands for anyone who would sell their rifle.

There were things happening all the time. I was accompanying the adjutant on a jeep with an escort, coming back from Sarafand, when we came across a lorry stopped in the road in front of us. Lying in their own blood were the army driver and his mate, dead. The Arabs who had done this ghastly deed were just finishing with the bodies. They saw us coming and ran. We stopped and our escort and I ran after them. They scattered, some on one side of the road and some on the other side. I chased two of them. One escaped. The other I shot dead and left him where he was in a waddi. I was so mad after seeing the two army blokes lying there. It was awful. When I chased the Arabs, I was still crying for them.

On our way back from the horrible scene, my adjutant turned to our driver as we approached the guard on the gates of our sister regiment, which he wanted to call on, on our way back to Rafah. He said to the driver, "Drive through. Let's see if they are alert." Because we should have stopped. So we sped past the guards and they rightfully shot at us, but thankfully missed us. Anyway, he finished his business and we were off back to our camp at Rafah. But he certainly gave us a scare. These officers did some daft things at times just to impress us. Well, he certainly did this time. I felt like shooting him myself.

There were some good times though; one day on the notice board there was a notice from the Padre saying that anyone who was interested could go with him to the Holy Places. I jumped at the chance and promptly put my name down to go. We first visited the Holy Sepulchre. To enter from the outside the only entrance was a very, very small door which at one time many years ago had been a very large entrance but had gradually, over the years of different occupations, had been reduced in size until now the only way you could enter was to stoop down practically on to your hands and knees. Once inside it felt very holy. It was dark except for many candles and it felt very cold too. We could only whisper our amazement to each other. All the statues were covered with paper money from all over the world and with jewels, rings and necklaces and some wristwatches that ordinary pilgrims had left. We eventually came to the grotto where you had to go on your knees to see the simple stone with a hole in its middle. I did put my hand down the hole. We visited the tomb which seemed to be white chalk inside. Then, after spending some time in prayer with the padre, we went to receive our certificate of pilgrimage from the keeper.

Outside again, we walked the Stations of the Cross to the next place of interest. We passed the Field of Skulls and also had pointed out to us the place where Pilate had interrogated Christ. I soon found myself on the Mount of Olives, with the same olive trees that Christ has known, and then to Gethsemane, which was again, to me, awe inspiring. At Gethsemane was yet another church. It just oozed sadness as you went through the doors. Once again, it was very silent, very gloomy with purple glass windows. Where there should have been an altar there was a large oblong piece of grey stone. All around the stone there was a low iron railing in the shape of thorns. It just took my breath away to stand there and take it all in. I did kneel and I uttered my prayers, but in silence. I just felt so privileged to be there. I will never forget all that I saw that day as long as I live.

We were soon, too soon, back in camp and I was getting ready for guard duty again with my Bren gun chained to my wrist. I climbed the steps into the lookout tower for another two hours. That was the duty: two hours on and two hours off in your bed then another two hours on etc all night long. It was on one of those nights that I was sitting with my back against the side facing the entrance to my tower. Steps! I could hear the officer coming up the steps, I pointed me Verey pistol, waiting for him to show. He came up the ladder and with his cane tapped my boots which were closer. "Are you awake, sentry?" he said. I said "If you do that again I'll blow your head off!" "Oh, well done" he said and descended the ladder again. He never bothered me again while he was duty officer.

We had a camp cinema there and while we were waiting for the films to start they played music to drown out the sporadic gunfire. One record they played over and over again, which I loved, was Roberto Inglesias and his orchestra playing Chopin's Fantasy Impromptu in Beguine tempo. On the other side of the record was Nocturne in E. I would give a lot to have that record now. I can't buy it anywhere. The cinema was very welcome in the army. Every regiment had one. Ours was in a corrugated iron hut, but, as I say, was very welcome.

We took our big guns out one day to show our strength to the Arabs and down one of the cactus flanked tracks we were ambushed and pinned down behind the cactus. One of our sergeants said, "Keep your heads down, lads", with machine bullets ricocheting off the big gun barrels. He then tried to get into the Matador truck and he was shot in the leg. We had to radio an infantry regiment to come and get us out of trouble. I think the regiment that rescued us was the King's Own Scottish Borderers (KOSB). We eventually managed to get our big guns out of there and returned to camp.

We had a wire fence all around the camp and we were detailed sometimes in our guard duty to patrol the fences. The nomad Arabs (we called them "wogs") would pester the guards to buy their wares. I saw a mate of mine being escorted by two police. I yelled, "What have you been up to?"

As I kept up with him and his escort, he replied, "I've shot one of the wogs. I told him I would if he didn't stop pestering me. Well, he wouldn't go away from the other side of the fence. So I shot him."

They took him away and I never saw him again.

On another occasion, we were driving through Haifa when we saw a garage where all these private cars were being driven in through one door and coming out of another door fully armoured. There was a very long queue of these cars waiting their turn.

We went to Mount Carmel to see what had been done to the St David Hotel, the one that was blown up by the Jews, and after many bad times of guard duties and different trips into danger, month after month, it was time for us to go on leave. We couldn't go home for our leave, but the powers that be had organized a holiday leave camp in Cyprus for all the forces stationed in Palestine.

One day, I was told that it was my turn to go, with many others from my regiment, which had been the 2nd Med but was now changed to the 39th Med, and other regiments, or from the Navy or Air Force. I was to board the corvette HMS Tripolitania at Haifa. I was given my hammock and told where I was to sling it to sleep.

It was late when we sailed from Haifa. I hadn't been long in my hammock when I started to itch. So I went up on deck. It was a nice warm evening and I found many others who had had the same idea as me, all lying on the deck. I managed to find a spot and laid out my hammock on the deck and got under my blanket. I spoke to a bloke on my right and we got talking. "Did you itch?" he asked. "Yes," I said. Then he told me that the ship we were on had been sunk twice and that was the reason for everyone's discomfort.

It was a long trip, but we should be in Famagusta the next day, he said. We were all pleased to leave the ship. There was transport in the form of army trucks all lined up on the dock to take us to our leave camp. And what a name they had given it! It was "The Golden Sands Holiday Camp", and it was very good. It was lovely to settle in, to go swimming in the lovely sea and run on the golden sands. There was great food; the billets were great and so were the bars. We were treated very well. I couldn't fault it on anything.

But I always liked to be on my own, so I decided to take myself off to Famagusta all on my own. My transport was a bicycle, which you could hire for a day. All you had to do was leave your AB64 PART (1)—your Army book. So off I went on a wonderful sunny day across a large field to the town.

I was standing outside a shop in the scorching sun, and the shopkeeper came out and brought a chair for me to sit on. They did this all the time. I had a look round and found a pub, and went in. There were four blokes sitting around a table. I was wondering what to do when from the badges on their uniforms I saw that they were Danish. I went to the table and introduced myself and we got chatting. They spoke a lot of English, so we could understand each other. One of them went to the bar with me to buy some drinks for all of us.

Well! When the bottles of beer were brought to the table, it was made in Denmark. The four Danes were ecstatic. They thought they were in Denmark. I'm sure they ordered a crate and put it under our table. We chatted and drank, and drank, and drank the lovely beer. I paid my way, of course, and a good time was had by all. They had also come from the Golden Sands Camp.

As the sun went down and the lights came on, we went our separate ways, the others still singing the Danish National Anthem. I wandered around the town. I saw a nice restaurant and had my fill, then went on my way exploring lovely Famagusta. I saw a throng of people all bunched together near a big posh car. Everyone was excited and the reason for the excitement was that a famous film star was in town, Turhan Bey. I had seen most of his films so I joined the crowd of happy people and even managed to talk to him and tell him the films I had seen which he had been in. The autograph came later.

Well, that was a treat for me! But now I was alone again and looking for the next bar. I found it and in it were some fellows I'd met on the ship. They asked me if I'd ever tried grappa. I said I hadn't but they told me it was great. So I asked the waiter to bring me "grappa, please" "Yes, sir". Along came a glass of water, a plate of nuts and salad, and something else (The name escapes me at the moment). Then came the grappa, a tiny drop in the bottom of a glass.

"You don't need all that stuff", they said. "Just drink the grappa. It will do you good". I knew then I was being taken for a ride, so I put the brakes on and took things very slowly. I could see they were all waiting to see me drink this "grappa". It just looked like water to me. Anyway, I had a tiny sip and I thought my head was going to explode. So I drank some water, ate all the nuts, and started on the salad.

We were all getting over the joke when the lads told me that we shouldn't be drinking it as it was a banned drink for His Majesty's Forces. Just then, a bloke from another table who had been trying it, stood up, shouted something and threw his chair at the window. At that point, I quickly left.

The sun was coming up and I realized I had been up all night. I had better get back to Camp Golden Sands right away. By the time I had retrieved my bicycle, it was daylight. Off I went, back across the fields, but on the way something else happened. There was a sandy track where I was happily cycling along when in front of me, across the track, was a huge black snake. I froze, then got off my bike and just stood there looking at this snake, with its tongue going in and out. It was like a python in its width, but black. I was very scared. I knew I had to get past it. But it wasn't about to go anywhere. I don't know how long I was there, but in the end I put my bike on my shoulder and stepped over the snake. I jumped on my bike and pedalled like mad. I gave my bike to the bloke I had got it from.

"Where have you been?" he said. "This should have been back yesterday."

I just said, "Give us my book." I took the book off him and collapsed. I came to on my bed in my billet. Every time I spoke to anyone for some time afterwards I was shooting them with peanuts from my mouth. I never touched grappa again. People drink grappa today but it's not as strong today. We had the real stuff.

There was always more exploring to do as I tried to see as much of Cyprus as I could before my two weeks leave was up and I would be back in Bomb Alley again. I took a bus to the mountain region and had a look around Troodos. It was very beautiful and the Cypriots were such nice people to know, very friendly people, I thought.

Well, I had had a lovely leave but it was time to go back to Haifa again, and then on to the Egyptian side of Palestine. Once I was back at Rafah again, there were more interesting trips on the Battery notice board. There was a trip to the Dead Sea, which was so buoyant you couldn't sink. Another time, there was a trip to Petra, a beautiful place where big what looked like palaces were built into the red rock. With the sunlight on it, it looked like fairyland. There were rock lizards darting about, as big as cats. They were huge!

Then all the talk was about the British Mandate coming to an end, and things were getting very bad. The numbers of Jews were increasing all the time. They set up kibbutzim to increase their population and appealed for more and more money for arms and anything the terrorists could use. We noticed how the Jews were getting very excited at the prospect of having their own state.

The ships coming into Haifa were full of Jewish immigrants from everywhere. The Navy couldn't stop them, and we had to deal with the influx. Their case for their own state was being discussed in the United Nations, and the British were gradually leaving, so the troops were getting fewer every day. The one day we were all gathered around the radio as the vote in the United Nations was being held. The terrorist Jews had won. They were given just a very small part of Palestine and the Palestinian Arabs had the rest.

We were to be the last to leave as the Egyptian Spitfires and tanks came roaring across the border. We were under fire from all this. We were all asked to drive anything out of Palestine. If you could ride a bike, you were given the keys to different vehicles, and told to take it to Egypt, leave it there and come back for another one. The Army were determined to get as much Army property out as they could in the short time they had left. Half the forces of occupation left by sea via Haifa and half by land via Rafah.

We went by land to Port Said, and then on by sea to Tripoli, which was to be our next station. "Tripoli" means "three camps". The name comes from Roman times. The three camps were Tripoli, Homs and Misratah, where we were stationed, was the furthest from Tripoli. As we were driven from the dock at Tripoli we passed the most famous Roman site, Leptis Magna. The ruins were, in some cases, better than in Rome itself. I saw them as we passed but was to visit them properly later, when we were settled.

We found ourselves in a nice barracks once more, and I loved the town. I even had a pet barn owl, Snowy White, a lovely bird. One day we were invited to Homs to meet a famous general from World War Two, William Slim, "Willie Slim" as we called him, from the war against the Japanese. I was so proud when he shook my hand. I had seen him many times in newsreels and knew of his exploits. In fact, had the Far Eastern war gone on, I might have been serving under him. But here he was in person, chatting to me, lucky me! We saw him at Homs, where our sister regiment was, 1st RHA. They invited us over there to see the great man.

Later on, we visited the famous Roman site at Leptis Magna. There was a lot to see there. The thing that was strange was that at the time when the site was occupied they had depended very much on the sea, but in 1948/9 you could not see the sea. It was nowhere to be seen. Yet in the days of the Romans they were sailing their ships from there. They had a central heating system and an elaborate sewage disposal system, all of which required the sea to operate. It was all there, the forum, the theatre, the market place and the arena where the chariot races took place. There was marble flooring everywhere. It was an exceptional site in every way. I spent a lot of time there. Every chance I got I went there to be amazed over and over again. I even found a well with the grooves showing where the ropes had been used over years to pull the buckets up, plain to see.

Back at the barracks in Misratah, when not on duty, I helped our padre to build—or rather make—a large room into our chapel. We had never had our own chapel, so it was good when it was finished, and it was appreciated, I am sure. The reason for my next problem was that there was a dental officer in town. I was detailed with many others to have a dental inspection. My teeth, to me, were all perfect, but this dental officer insisted they all had to come out. I protested in vain. To make matters worse, he left half of my tooth in there. He had broken my tooth, trying to take a perfectly good tooth out. I think, in hindsight, he had to fullfil his quota. Anyway, he had me in agony for a few weeks.

Then something else happened. The British Military Hospital in Tripoli was short of nurses, and I was asked if I would "Volunteer" to be sent to Tripoli hospital to be trained as a nurse. I said yes, I would, and I was off on a further adventure. There was an urgent need for more nurses because they couldn't get an intake from the Royal Army Medical Corps, so they sent to other regiments like ours.

It must have been very urgent, because as soon as I agreed to go, I was packing my kit and being driven to beautiful Tripoli. What a really nice hospital that was, from the regime of Mussolini. He was responsible for this beautiful building and I felt quite good to be a part of such a hospital. I was introduced to five lads who were in the Medical Corps and had been at the hospital for a long time. They tried to frighten me with stories at first, but I was very soon accepted and befriended by them. I was introduced to some of my patients and shown over the wards and the operating theatre. I met some very nice Royal Alexandra nurses, and there were some very attractive girls among them. I thought I had hit the jackpot, but that would change.

The work was very interesting but very hard. I was soon taking care of people, or I should say guardsmen, from the Grenadier Guards, the Irish Guards and the Coldstream Guards. These were some of the many regiments stationed in Tripoli, as well as the American GIs. My first ward after training and passing my test was the Ear, Nose and Throat (ENT). I had to administer penicillin injections and dispense alcohol, as well as assisting on other wards when needed. They were very busy days and would get a lot busier as time went on. I had to do day duty and night duty and assist in the operating theatre as well as the mortuary, and with the mental patients.

It made me realize just what splendid work a nurse has to do. Also, before you come off night duty you have to write a report for the day sister to keep up to date with everything. If there was a night sister, she would write her report from your report. The night work was not too bad if you were very busy, but if not, then it was a very long night. I remember one night I was on the ward with the mental patients. A lady patient was telling me a tale. She said she had had a visitor, whom I had just missed because he had just jumped out of the window. I knew the windows were secure, but I promised her I would go outside to see if he was all right. Of course, there was no-one there.

Christmas was upon us, and plans were being made by the lads I was with in our billet in the hospital grounds, when we got together, which wasn't often. The lads were discussing decorating the room we lived and slept in. They were complaining that we had no decorations so I promised to get some somehow. With a few toilet rolls and some coloured paints I turned the toilet rolls into decorations and this is how we improvised. There was plenty of cotton wool for snow. So we had a Christmas tree. We just took a branch from one of the many small trees in the grounds and decorated it with cotton wool and all kinds of small things. We painted some bits. It all looked great and we were all pleased with our efforts. Some of the other staff said how good the room looked for Christmas. We sang carols for our patients and we were such a good choir with the female nurses we were much appreciated. We made Christmas mean something to the lads lying in their beds.

Some were very sick indeed because a sort of plague had descended on the Guards department in Tripoli, in the form of a disease called poliomyelitis. It was very bad. We were constantly admitting soldiers from the various Guards regiments with the disease. This was a fatal disease. What it did to these Guardsmen was to paralyse them. First, their feet were paralysed and then their legs, then gradually moving upwards. So, what we had to do, as soon as it affected their breathing, was quickly put them into one of the two iron lungs we had at the hospital, then give them continuous injections while they were in the iron lung. But, one after another, they died. We were losing them every day, sometimes two a day. Nobody seemed to know anything about it. It was a new disease. We had a man from the Irish guards who refused to die. He should have stayed in his bed but he kept getting out and running up and down the ward. He was the first man to be released cured. But overall it was terrible: all those lives we couldn't save, so many healthy young Guardsmen, gone.

Gradually we got on top of this new disease and there were fewer and fewer deaths until they found the source of the disease, and the carrier. They obviously did this, because the deaths stopped, thank goodness, and things for a while were better. This was only for a few months because then there was a bigger catastrophe. Two aircraft, both carrying troops, crashed into each other, one taking off from Tripoli airport and the other landing, bringing troops from the Far East. It was all hands to the pumps, as dozens of injured, dead and dying soldiers were brought to the hospital for us to deal with. The Alexandra nurses were excellent in a crisis, which this certainly was. First, I was wheeling injured troops to the theatre; next, I was wheeling a barrow load of limbs to the lift up to the roof, where the incinerator was. I worked until I collapsed myself and was put to bed in the hospital. I had pleurisy and pneumonia.

The thing that happened to me next was very strange. I must have been unconscious for some time when I suddenly woke up in the middle of the night. The ward was quiet. I could see the night nurse sitting at the desk at the end of the ward, by her small light, but the rest of the ward was also lit. It was filled by a bright light, bright enough to read a newspaper by, although all the lights had been turned off for the night. I suddenly realized the light source was a tiny little ball giving off this blue white light. It just hung there in mid air, hovering. I could see everything in the ward so clearly.

This was the start of my recovery, and I soon got better after this—whatever it was. However, years later, I was working on a building site in Cheapside, London, when the foreman on the job realized I couldn't hear. He sent me to St Bartholomew's Hospital to have my ears syringed. While I was there, I found there was a lovely chapel to St Bartholomew in the grounds. I picked up a leaflet on my way out of the chapel, which was very lovely inside. I had gone in to pray, as I usually do when visiting a place that is holy. As I had more time to wait for the treatment for my deafness, I sat on a bench in the sun in the grounds of the chapel.

I couldn't believe what I was reading. The leaflet said that Bartholomew was in Italy when he became very ill. He then had the very same experience as I had had in the hospital in Tripoli of the little blue light hanging in the air. When he saw the light he was cured of his illness. He thought it was a miracle, so when he returned to London he built this chapel. Even as I sit here, writing this, I can feel cold shivers up and down my back. There are many things like this that I can't explain, but this was my experience, the same as St Bartholomew's.

As I quickly recovered, they gave me some convalescence time. I took the opportunity to see more of Tripoli. I was near the dock, and there was a huge aircraft carrier right there in front of me. They were unloading a beautiful American car on to the dock by means of the ship's crane. There on the dock was the Tripoli Museum, so I took myself in. I like museums.

When I came out, a ball, an American football, landed at my feet. It had come from the deck of the aircraft carrier, the Franklin D. Roosevelt. I looked up. The American servicemen were asking me to come aboard and bring the ball with me. There were several gangplanks leading up. I chose one and made my way up to the flight deck. I was met halfway by an American sailor who explained that they were playing football on the flight deck and asked whether I would like to go up to the deck. I had nothing else to do and I love warships. So that was another nice episode in my interesting life. It was good to talk to the Yanks and exchange stories about our different experiences.

It was soon time to go, so, with gum in my mouth and American Camel cigarettes in my pocket, I left the ship and continued my tour of the town. After I had visited a nice restaurant and once again had Pasta Chuta, I went for a walk with someone I had met in the restaurant. I was thinking about how hot it can get in Tripoli and my companion said, "You haven't been to Garian, have you?"

"No, I haven't."

"Well, if you went there today, you could get frostbite."

Garian looks down on Tripoli from many miles above sea level. That is why it is so cold, as I was to find out.

When I got back from my period of convalescence, I was soon put back to work in the hospital. There were still a lot of men from the air crash needing treatment, so there was plenty of work to do. I soon got back to what I did best, and that was making people better after their illnesses. It was lovely to feel appreciated again, which I was. Without bragging too much, I was good at my new occupation and was enjoying my work, which always helps you to do well.

I was told that I would be on ambulance duty and would be accompanying some regiment to, of all places, Garian. So I would experience the frostbite for myself. These regiments did their manoeuvres on the Heights of Garian, and had to have at least one ambulance with them. So, off we drove, up, up to Garian, the higher we went up the mountain road. When we parked, I remembered that the female nurses had asked me to bring them something back, the tiny wild tortoises, which were very attractive to the girls. I wandered about the rocks and saw loads of them, so it was very easy to pick them up and put them in a sack I had brought with me.

I asked the driver and the other chap about the frostbite. They explained that it was mostly when the sun went down. They said that's why the nomad people here live underground. They call them "trogs", or troglodytes, because they live in subterranean dwellings. We had a bit of free time, so I was determined to see for myself. I wandered across the flat land for about half a mile away from where the ambulance was, and I came to a hole about a hundred yards wide. Just off the rim of this large hole were smaller holes with steps cut out of the soil. These steps led down to a single cave-like dwelling. There were these Berber families living very nice and comfortable lives.

I was invited in and made very welcome with a very small cup of tea. It was nice and warm underground, and these dwellings were everywhere. How they managed to cut these large holes I'll never know. They were so large and deep, they were beyond belief. I said my goodbyes and made my way back to the ambulance before the sun went down. It was turning cold when I got back. I saw that the tortoises were okay, and then settled down to get some shut-eye before the night—gunners' exercise began. I was on duty that night. So when the sun shone, the next morning. I could be on my way exploring again. I paid last visit to the troglodytes, and then continued to walk across the fields, and that is where I came across another interesting sight.

It seems that in World War II, the Yanks had passed this way, and they had kept but a reminder of the fact in a wonderful painting of a naked young lady. This was in Garian, and the painting took up most of a wall. Her body was a sort of map of where they had fought their battles. There were images of columns of troops walking all over her, and trucks and tanks and German guns. It was amazing. It was called "The lady of Garian". In a shop in Tripoli. I even bought a picture of it later on.

Well, after the army games had come to an end, I returned to the hospital and to what I do best, looking after the sick. We had an

American officer come in. We had to put him in a ward of his own. He was very ill, but we put him in an oxygen tent and gave him the different injections prescribed by my officer. But nothing we were doing was having much effect on his illness. I had been reading in a newspaper or a journal like "The Lancet" about people in America, trying out a new drug. I think it was called streptomycin. I mentioned this to my officer over a break time cup of tea. The next thing that happened was that he told me we would give him this drug. I said, "You'd have to go to America to get it".

He said he'd been in touch with his unit in Tripoli, and they were sending a big Flying Fortress to America to get this drug for my sick American officer. And from what I heard they did just that and I was soon injecting my sick officer with the new drug. He got better and was discharged. My officer in charge at the hospital got all kinds of honours from the Americans, and I myself got a very nice thank you, with a handshake, from my officer.

Years later, I was in Oxford Street in London, out shopping with my wife, Cynthia, when a man ran from the other side of the road towards me. I wondered what he was doing and whether it was m he was running towards. Catching his breath, he said, "I thought it was you. You made me well when I was in the hospital in Tripoli". He said, "I am always telling my wife about you. There she is, across the road. Would you come to meet her?"

"Of course," I said. "I would be honoured," and he went to help her across the road. She said, "It's lovely to meet you. He's never stopped talking about you, and the time he was in hospital in Tripoli". My wife was a bit surprised at all this adoration I was receiving, but not as surprised as I was. It was nice of him to remember me, but with so many men I had to nurse, I honestly couldn't remember him, but then, I never had favourites. They all needed my care and to the best of my knowledge, they all received it.

Well, I loved my time at the hospital in Tripoli, but I knew I couldn't stay there, however much I wanted to. I knew someday it would come to an end. After all, I was an artillery man in an artillery regiment, not one of the Royal Medical Corps. It was sad as I said my goodbyes, and as I departed on a bright sunny Sunday morning. We went past the married quarters, and there in his garden was our senior surgeon sawing a small log of wood. It was strange, because on the night of the air crash, I had witnessed him sawing a man's lower limb off, and here he was doing the same to a part of a tree.

Well, goodbye Tripoli! Hello again, Misratah! But I wasn't back very long before I was sent home on the demob leave. I had served the King for eight years. I had signed up for seven years with the colours and five years in reserve. But I had done eight with the colours and four reserve. So, I soon found myself back in Port Said again, waiting for the ship to take me home, and it couldn't have been at a worse time. The regimental sergeant major had been responsible for the death of a soldier back in Blighty in an army detention centre and the powers that be had simply sent him to Egypt to put him in charge of the Port Said transit camp.

This man was a walking maniac. What he did at the camp was mind boggling. He had a stores full of brand new webbing equipment and brand-new rifles. He is orders were that everyone who passed through the transit camp would have to do guard duty. And he had his officers and non-commissioned officers to mount on the parade ground, two complete guard complements, not one. The reason he gave was that if one complement of guard failed the inspection, he would change them, and mount the other complements of guard. But that's not all. You see, every man of the two guards' complements had to draw new web being equipment and a new rifle. The most difficult equipment to clean and Blanco for guard duty is brand new equipment, with all the brass fittings on the webbing equipment. And then there was the rifle. When it is brand new it's full of grease.

All this cleaning and polishing boots to see your face in and getting your uniform all pressed took all day to do. We then had to mount guard for the night. All of us were just waiting for a ship to take us on leave, away from there. The man was a nutter! At the same time, there was an epidemic of cholera in Egypt, and we had all had injections before leaving our units, and on arrival at Port Said.

I had a bit of a personal confrontation with this sergeant major in as much as, when my guard's complement had passed the rigorous inspection, I was put on guard in the section where the sergeant major's private house was. It was close to the outside of the camp, and there were some Arab youths throwing stones at his house. Although it was happening where I shouldn't walk, I thought it my duty to inform him about what these youths were doing. As I approached his lodge, he came towards me, very angry at my being on his property. I tried to explain but he just told me to get back on duty, where I should be.

As luck would have it, a ship arrived at Port Said, and nothing had been reported about the incident. So there were to be no more guards at Port Said for me. But it wasn't the end of my duties for on the SS Dunera I was put to work again. I had to join the sick bay attendant in injecting the crew and many of the passengers against cholera. My nursing experience was coming in handy for the ship.

It was a lovely crossing at first. As we made our way to Malta, and then on to Gibraltar, we hit some really bad weather. The ship was lost in the Bay of Biscay for three days. In fact, they were running bets on who would be the first passenger or member of the crew to be right about where we were.

We eventually docked at Liverpool and disembarked. Then, we were into trucks to take us to Huyton transit camp. I wanted to go home instead of spending time at the transit camp, because I could have gone to my sister's, who was living in Liverpool. But everyone in that camp at Huyton went home before me because I had to give more injections against cholera.

Eventually, I got home to my sister's. They were pleased to see me and she said our ship had been the talk of Liverpool with it is being lost. She showed me the news of the event being published in pictures and pages and pages of the Liverpool Echo. While I had been in touch with my sister, I had asked her to try to get a record of Frank Sinatra singing "Stella by Starlight". When I got to my sister's, she said, "I've got your record". I was so pleased, and in her excitement wanting to let me hear it, she broke it. In those days, the shopkeepers used to put raffia through the hole in the centre of the record. She had tried to snap the raffia instead of cutting it with scissors. Well, when she told me she had broken the record, I lost it and I swore the "F" word. I was so ashamed, I took myself out, and didn't come back until nighttime to say I was very sorry to my sister.

But there were nice days afterwards. She and her husband made a fuss of me for my leave, and I felt very grateful to them both. I took my younger sister and her young sister out to the Paramount Cinema. It was very posh in those days. Then we went on to a nice restaurant. I gave them a nice time. I remember my sister liked, or was a fan of, a film star called Guy Madison, and he was in the film we saw. I think it was called "As Time Goes By", or "Till the End of Time", something like that, anyway. So there were nice days together with what was left of our family.

I said my goodbyes to my sister after my leave came to an end. I thanked her, said goodbye to my two dear younger sisters, and left for London and my next posting before I was to leave the army. This posting was in a place in Essex called Shoeburyness. The train journey took me to Euston railway station in London, then by Underground to Fenchurch Street railway station.

It was quite late by the time I found somewhere in London to have a meal before boarding a train to Fenchurch Street for Shoeburyness. I arrived there in pitch darkness and thought, "Where the hell have they sent me to?" I couldn't go any further. It was the end of the line. I gathered my kit together and started to walk out of the station. I asked the ticket collector where the barracks were and he gave me directions.

When I got there, I reported to the guardroom and after a while I was escorted to C Block. Up the stairs I went to find my room and bed. Each bed had a nice tall locker beside it and all the blokes except one were fast asleep. As I was putting my kit away, I was mumbling under my breath about the rotten place I had been sent to, when the bloke beside me asked, "Do you like Blackpool?".

"Yes," I answered.

"Well," he said, "It's better than that, two miles up the road from here. Wait and see. Now get to bed and stop your bloody moaning."

So that's what I did. I awoke to the bugle call "Reveille" and was amazed to see the lads all dressing in Navy whites, bellbottoms and all. I thought I was back on the HMS Liverpool. I had to collect my Navy whites, and I had an interview with the adjutant. He explained to me that what I would be doing here was To Secret and the reason for the Navy whites was so I would be seen when I was way out on the sand, marking where the shells and munitions had fallen after the guns had fired them. I was now, he said, an XP. He explained that this place was a Proof and Experimental Establishment, and I was now working for the Ministry of Supply, a top government department. Having taken all this in, I was driven to the artillery ranges and a Sergeant Major, told me to enter a brick built office.

I went in and was given or rather shown a copy of the Official Secrets Act, which I had to sign. Then they took my fingerprints and details of my two tattoos, and asked me to make out a will. To be honest, I was getting quite excited about my new posting. Then, the Sergeant Major said, "You could do with a cup of tea". He told me the NAAFI would be along any minute now. Then there it was, a box on wheels. Well, that's what it looked like, but it was much more than that.

There was a man who drove the trolley, or whatever it was, and he served the tea and cakes or buns from this NAAFI on the railway truck. It was welcomed by all.

I sat down on an ammunition box with the Sergeant Major who enlightened me about the rules here. He said, "You will be chatting to admirals, generals, politicians and even Royalty. Here, that is normal. And there will be no saluting. Saluting is not required here.

That was understandable, because you would be saluting every single minute. Everyone was there, except Winston Churchill. I have never seen so many of the highest ranking officers in my life, and you could sit and chat with them if they asked you a question. It seemed they were human beings after all.

My first job was to be assigned to one of the many big guns. The first one I was on was anti-aircraft gun, a 3.7, I believe it was. But we only pointed it down range not up in the air. We fired this gun most of that day and each time we fired we would recognise the high-ranking officer. It would go something like this: I, with my finger on the trigger behind a metal screen, would say, "Right the gun, Sir." He, the officer, would reply, "Ready?" I would reply, "Right, Sir." Then, the officer would say, "Fire!"

Then I would pull the trigger, and there would be our mighty bang. With other guns firing as well, there was plenty of noise. When we finished firing for the day, they would send the DRABYs out on the beach. The DRABYs were large horse-drawn carts. They were used to collect shells and ammunition and bring them back to be analysed by the scientists, and physicists who came with the generals, admirals or Wing Commanders.

There were many new inventions being tried out for the first time. I was told that before D-Day scientists were dropped over Normandy to bring back samples of the German defences. We would make a replica wall, and then find out what would destroy it. That was down to the XPs, here in Shoeburyness, Essex. Well, I couldn't wait to see if I was on guard duty yet. I checked, the notice board and to my delight. It wasn't yet my turn.

So my first evening of freedom was here. I was ready to find out what this Shangri La that was letter than Blackpool was like. The bloke who was in the next read to me I had soon made my mate. As luck would have it, he wasn't on guard duty, either. So, best bib and tucker, on, we would go to Southend on Sea together, the Shangri La. But first, there was a lovely pub right outside the gate to the barrack complex.

"Very handy," I said. "What are you having?" Pricey, my mate was. He was Taffy Price, a Welshman. While I was drinking my pint, I noticed a bloke in uniform like mine, who looked the image of Robert Mitchum. I suppose that explained all the young girls around him. Anyway, Taffy and I left the pub and made our way to the bus stop for Southend.

He was right. It was just like Blackpool. The bus stopped at the seafront, with the longest pier in the world not too far away. But first, we went into the pub. It was great inside, full of squaddies and lovely girls and a band whose compere today would be called "gay", if you know what I mean, but he was very good at his job. We all loved him and he greeted us all. It was wonderful in there. We were soon chatting, the girls up.

Coming out of the pub, we saw the biggest fairground I've ever seen called the Kursaal. We had a got out a few of the rides and on some of the stalls, like coconut shies, were good as well. So me and Taff were living it up. All along the seafront, where we went there were arcades and pubs and all the music and singing and sounds of laughter coming out, of all of them.

On pub, I remember, was called "The Army and Navy", and it was full to the rafters, as they say. So, we were bound to pay this one a visit. We finally got to the bar and stood there. I was standing next to this woman and I started to chat with her. I said, "You look exactly like Hermione Gingold". She whispered to me not to say that too loudly as she was Hermione Gingold. I realised she was telling the truth when the chap with her told me to get lost. In his, jacket he was wearing a gun. So I was about to get lose when Hermione said to him, "No, leave him. He's all right." So we started a nice conversation, and it was wonderful to think who had bought me a drink.

She was wonderful to talk to, and I enjoyed her company very much after she had brought her bodyguard in his place. She left with a fond goodbye. Taff and I left soon after, as he wanted to show me where some other places were like cafes and cinemas. There was the famous Gar on name all over the place. It seemed like he owned quite a bit of Southend.

There were plenty of cinemas, and one which only showed good old films like those with Bogart and Bette Davis. I think they were all Warner Bros films. The price to go in was only one shilling. It was a wonderful little cinema which, later on, I would visit very often, but not that night. We just walked off, Taff and I, and eventually we called it a day.

So, it was back to the barracks at Shoeburyness. We were soon tucked up in our beds and chatting about what we had done. Taff mentioned that you could make money in Southend by a working on the rides in the Kursaal, or by making ice cream in Rossi's. So, with this in mind, I fell asleep until Reveille brought me back to the old routine on the ranges, with a different job this time.

I had to carry sticks of explosive cordite. It looked like spaghetti, as you buy it in the shop before it is cooked. Well, the cordite, if you can imagine, was stored in brick buildings all over the gun range. You had it stored from side to side of the building from the floor to the ceiling with a narrow passage running through the middle. The passage through the middle was only wide enough for one man to walk through, with the sticks of cordite almost touching each shoulder. So, it was single file, carrying cordite on your shoulder, in one door, deposit the cordite, and out the far door.

Well, with all this explosive on both sides, and with my load and the blokes in front and behind you were saying your prayers all the way. I turned around, because I could smell smoke, and to my horror the man behind me had a fag lit in his mouth. What fright we all had in there. No one said anything because I think his punishment would have been very hard, and after all, we were all still alive. When we got out we made sure that didn't happen again, on our shift.

But that is just one of many scary happenings. Another time, we were to witness the dropping of a huge bomb, with the Air Force officers carrying this out. The bomb was hoisted up to a certain height, and then would be lowered slowly back to the ground. It must have been an important exercise, because they had about a hundred of us sitting in a huge circle around this bomb, which was high above us. Suddenly, the bomb dropped and we all, including the officers, scattered as fast as we could. We thought that was the end. However, it didn't explode, as you must know, and the officer in charge simply said, "Sorry chaps, that wasn't supposed to happen."

Well, that was the end of another not so perfect day, and to make it worse, I was detailed for guard duty. But Taff said, because he wasn't on guard duty, "Scouse, there's a bike behind the green shed if you want it." I heard that some of the lads used the bike to go to work at Rossi's or the Kursaal while being on guard duty. They would wait until the duty officer had been around the guard, and then go to work in Southend. So I gave it a try and made myself a few pounds, making ice cream. That bike was certainly made use of.

One day, I made some money without realising it. I was detailed to be part of a guard of honour at a funeral. After I had fired my salute over the grave, I walked, or marched, away. The undertaker was hiding behind a tree in the graveyard, and as we marched past him, he gave us all a bit of cash. It was the garrison church, so I suppose it was custom.

Another day, I was chosen to be part of the gun crew to fire the biggest gun of a size I'd only seen in the movies. It was taken from a battleship, 15 or 18 inch, but very big. You could crawl down the barrel, it was so big. Of course, it was mounted on the railway line, and they told me this was how they had destroyed Hitler's western wall. They perfected the shells here before they were loaded on to battleships on D-Day. This was Shoeburyness in all its glory but I didn't know the next chapter that was coming while I was in Southend, one day, all alone, as I often liked to be.

Meeting Betty

I mentioned the Garon cinema before but right there with the cinema was a restaurant, also called Garon's. I went into this restaurant and sat down at an empty table, that is to say no one else was sitting at the table. Within a few minutes there was this lovely waitress standing there with her pad and pencil at the ready to take my order. She had on a lovely uniform, a nice little hat on her long fair hair, a white pinny over her sky blue skirt and top with long sleeves of sky blue, starched white cuffs and collar.

Then she spoke in a slight Scottish accent, "Yes, sir?" I asked for a tea and toasted teacake. "Thank you, sir," and off she went to get what I had ordered. I couldn't wait for her to return. It must have been love or something, because I was looking out for her coming back. Anyway, the tea and toasted teacake were very nice. I ate the cake as slowly as I could. I just didn't want to leave. She came past my table again and gave me a lovely smile. "Is there anything else, sir?" she said. I realised I'd been in the restaurant quite a while for a tea and teacake customer. So, not wanting to leave, I called her over and gave a repeat order.

She brought it over and said, "We don't get many XPs in here. Have you been with them long?"

"No, not long", I replied, "I'm just here till I get demobbed. I'm home from abroad".

"I thought you had a nice colour," she said. "I thought you must have been sunbathing."

I couldn't believe what she said next.

"I'm off work in about twenty minutes," she said. "If you come back, I'll show you Southend."

"What's your name?" I asked.

"Betty."

Well I came back later, and waited outside for a while, but I could see her inside and she pointed to her wristwatch and then showed me five fingers. In next to no time, we were together, and to she looked nice in the town clothes with gloves and handbag to match. "Well," she said, "What's your name?"

I said, "Alfred."

"Oh," she said, "that's too posh. I'll call you Alf." Then she linked her arm through mine, and we walked back towards the river. I must be dreaming, I thought, because when I first saw her I didn't think she would give me a second look. And yet here we were as if we had been going out with each other for years. We walked along the front, but not the side with all the pubs. She called it the West Cliff side because the next place, along there was called West Cliff. She said it was the posh part, and it was where all the Jews lived. I said, "Are you a Jew?"

"God, no," she said. "But quite a few come into the restaurant."

Well, we were walking and chatting, and then she said, "Here we are." I didn't realise she meant she was at her home. But then, thinking about it, when you finish work you go home. She opened her door and led me in as if I'd been there many times before.

"Hello, Mam," she hollered, as her mother came out of the small scullery, wiping her hands on her pinny.

"Where have you been, you naughty girl? Your dinner will be spoilt."

"Oh," I said. "That's my fault. I am new to Southend. Well, I'm new to Essex altogether, and your daughter kindly has been showing me around. I do apologise if I kept her out."

"No, that's all right. Sit down, son. I'll get you something to eat. Tea?"

"Yes, please, Mrs. Little." Later, my Betty took me to a pub called the cricketers, and then having discussed another meeting she took me to the bus stop for Shoeburyness. I did hand springs, all the way to the barrier. That's what I felt like doing, anyway. Goodnight, my love, I thought.

Well, we struck up a wonderful friendship. We were regulars at the Cricketers, but let me stress it wasn't for the drinking, but for the dancing. She liked to dance with me. So we made a nice dancing couple on the floor, on the dance floor, that is. She showed me lots of places in Southend-on-Sea, and in the same road that she lived with her family, that is, Princess Street, there was a spiritualist medium living and Betty, my now girlfriend was interested in spiritualism.

Well, one day or evening, we went to visit this lady and Betty said that I should have a reading. So, to please, Betty I did. First, to my surprise, that lady said I would get married and have five children. Well, I sit here writing this, and I am the father of five children, but that's a story for later.

We didn't talk marriage. We had only just met, and it was very good. We would visit the Kursaal fun fair, sometimes, and, another time, walk along the longest pier in the world. We would go to the cinema together, and we did get on very well. While she was at work, waiting on tables in Garon's, I would sit having my cup of tea and toasted teacake, just watching her slipped from table to table. She looked lovely in her uniform, and she would smile at me as she went past the table I was sitting at. She knew a lot of her customers. I remember her telling me about a couple of very elderly people a lady and gentleman. She was talking with them at a table not far from the one I was sitting at, and she came from them to tell me they had invited the two of us to their home in Prittlewell, the next Sunday for lunch and on my behalf she had accepted.

I glanced past her at this couple who started waved to me. I waved back, and it was lovely to see how many of her customers like her. I finished my usual toasted teacake and left. I came back when she was due to finish, and waited for her, as usual, outside the restaurant. Then she explained how the couple had been coming there for ages. They were both in their nineties, she said. "But they looked so well", I said. "Yes," she smiled. "But he has never worked. He was a gambler on the horses, and that's how he made his money, backing horses.' Well, I couldn't wait to meet this man. He sounded very interesting, but I would have to wait until Sunday.

We went back to her house and I was introduced to the family, the rest of the family, that is, her older sister, Flo, who was a sergeant in the ATS, just arrived on leave, her older brother, Keith, who was very bright and studying to be a solicitor, and her younger sister, Jean, as well, of course, as her father, who was an ex-army regimental sergeant major. By his photograph in uniform, he looked a real terror. He was a Scotsman, from Dumfries. When I met him, I found his accent was very broad Scots. He was a very famous min in army circles, because he had founded the R.E.M.E. from the Royal Engineers. So among all these very clever people, I felt quite insignificant. I couldn't wait to finish my wonderful Scottish meal and wait for a Betty to get ready so that we could go out on the town again. I must say though that her family were very friendly towards me. Her mother came from London, but the children had all been born in Dumfries, and the moved to Essex. Even my Betty had a slight Scottish accent and was very proud of it. How mother being a Londoner, used to go to see her relations in London. I think it was in Battersea they lived. She promised to take Betty and me, one day soon to the famous Petticoat Lane Street market in London.

I looked forward to that and Betty had said, "You will love it!" Luckily, I wasn't delegated for guard duty. So we were able to keep our date to visit to the elderly couple from Prittlewell. The sun shone on us as we approached their front door. It was a strange sort of accommodation they lived in. The door was squeezed between two shops. Betty had not been there before, so she was as bemused as I was. We heard footsteps descending stairs, and then the door opened to reveal the elderly gentleman.

"Come in, dear," he said to Betty and all three of us ascended the stairs. At the top of the stairs was the door. We went through into a quaint small living room with lots of photographs of adorning the walls and sideboard, very dark wallpaper, and with the doors also a dark varnished colour. There was a nice fireplace with a mantelpiece and a large table in the middle of the room. On the table were lots of Racing Gazettes and lots of coloured pencils. I was fascinated as the gentleman started to explain his system of making a very good living by using his system, and he had done this for years and years.

The first thing he said made some sense to me. "It is a club of jockeys. They get together and decide whose turn it is to win." This was only for the small events, not the big races like the Derby or the Grand National or big events like those. Then I said, "So how do you know which horse will win?"

"Well," he explained, "You see here in this racing paper where it gives the names of owners and jockeys and such? Well, you read aloud the line till you see where that horse came in the last few races, if it came third or fourth or first or second. Well, here—you see this horse hasn't won since—so now you check the back issues of the Gazette, and you know by the coloured marks on the paper where the horse finished, because you have marked it in different colours. Red means it had come in first, and so on. Then you can say, with almost certainty, where he will finish today, because it is that jockey's turn to win. So you back him. And that's been my racing life."

Then he opened the door to another room, and in a wardrobe we saw the most wonderful suits of clothes, all from Savile Row. There were all his binoculars and down at the bottom were rows of wonderful, highly polished shoes and boots all lined up. It looked like the wardrobe of a millionaire, and perhaps it was, who knows?

Before we left, we had enjoyed a lovely salad lunch, and more conversations, Betty with the lady of the house, and I with the gentleman. He gave me the name of a horse to back that time, and it won, but not being a gambler myself, I didn't back it. But yes it did win! Well, that was wonderful, and they were a lovely couple, whom I often saw afterwards in the restaurant.

The gunnery went on every day, with me dressed in Navy whites, rubbing shoulders with the elite of the armed services and government. But it was the end of the day I looked forward to now, when I could hold my Betty in my arms again. We met as often as we could and even went on our day out at Petticoat Lane as had been promised to us by Betty's mother. The noise there in the street market was something to remember for the rest of your life and the colours of the different goods on display were something to behold. It was very cosmopolitan. I remember, with people of all nations trying to buy something that was considered a bargain. We even saw the pearly king and queen there. We bought a few things, but I don't remember what they were now. A wonderful day out in the sunshine was had by all of us. Then came the underground and Fenchurch Street station, and we were soon back at Southend for Betty, though, I stayed on the train, and in a couple of stops was back in Shoeburyness and my barracks.

As time went on, there was talk of my getting demobbed from the army, meaning demobilised and back to Civvy Street. At the same time, there was talk with her parents of marriage with my Betty. The talk got more often about our getting married. The reception should be in the British Legion Hall, I heard someone say. I wasn't supposed to hear things like that. And of course Betty was getting more excited. I told her I had to go and see my brother in Kingston on Thames soon and have a talk with him.

My Betty was now looking forward to what we must do and what she would wear. I said I could get married in my uniform, but she didn't want that. I was to have a new suit, and so that was arranged. Our honeymoon was to be in the house next door, but after that, we would have to find somewhere else to live. It had better be Shoeburyness, as I would still be in the army.

Well, the date was set for 22nd September and, my goodness, everything went so quickly then, right up to the "as long as we both shall live" bit in the ceremony. I truly meant those words. It was a beautiful wedding in the church at Prittlewell, with the wedding reception at the British Legion Hall, Victoria Avenue, Southend-on-Sea. We danced as did the hundred people who attended our beautiful wedding. Betty it was all in a beautiful white wedding dress with tiara, veil and train, and her tall, dark and handsome groom beside her.

The night seemed to go on forever. Eventually, we were driven back to the house next door to where Betty and her family lived. We were escorted to the bridal chamber, and it was "goodnight, folks!" I don't know what time it was when we were awakened by a lady with a gray of goodies, that is, two cups of tea and some toast, and I think orange juice and a sprig of flowers. At that moment, we could have been in Monte Carlo, it felt so good. We went back to Betty's house for our proper breakfast and then we went house hunting, or I should say room hunting.

We took a bus to Shoeburyness and found a very nice lady who was letting the room and was quite aware how we were feeling as newlyweds. She greeted us and made us feel welcome and and we sat and enjoyed her tea and biscuits as we discussed terms. She did tell us that she lived there alone, and that she was a member of the Southend ladies choir. She also mentioned that she owned a beach hut that she said we could use. Then she showed us the bed we would be sleeping in and the other contents of the room and adjoining bathroom and toilet. She laid down the rules with a firm hand, and then we left her, having accepted her offer of this nice accommodation. It wasn't very far from my barracks, but it was a bus ride to Betty's job; but she didn't seem to mind about that.

We so moved in to our new accommodation in Richmond Avenue, Shoeburyness, and it was soon our lovely home. Our landlady would go out quite a lot, and leave us in charge of her lovely house and her living room downstairs with her radio and all her lovely ornaments and pictures, which I admired. Those days were the happiest days I'd ever known. It was lovely, all the time, to be the husband to my dearest Betty. I was still in the army, and we still enjoyed dancing at the barracks every now and then. My days on the ranges continued still with my mates, but each evening, if I wasn't on guard duty, I would be home with my Betty.

I recall once being in the cookhouse for a while, and moving a big cardboard box—it was so light I couldn't believe it was full of cornflakes—and one day, we had two of those boxes by mistakes. The Sergeant said, "I don't know what to do with the other box". I said, "I'll get rid of it for you", so I put it on one shoulder, and it felt easy to ride my bike home like that. So I took a chance. I had to ride my bike to the radar tower and through the guards (military policemen) at the entrance to the ranges.

"What have you got there?"

"An empty box", I said. "I am taking it home. We have some packing to do, and it's just what I need."

"Okay, son, off you go."

And I rode home with this big box of cornflakes and my wife couldn't believe it. Anyway, when never went short of cornflakes for ages. Or our landlady. Or Betty's mum.

In time, I was told my army life was coming to an end. They said I would still be in the reserves, if the country ever needed me, and, before I knew it, I was sent for by the adjutant, who thanked me for my services, but then spelt out the instructions for demobilisation. He asked me if I had a job in mind for Civvy Street. I said I would like to be a policeman with the Met.

"Good for you", he said. "I think you will make a fine policeman. Have you enjoyed your stay with us?" To which I said, "Yes, sir!" He then said, "I will be giving you a good conduct report and arranging for you to join the police force. Good luck!" And off I went, after eight years in his Majesty's forces, into the unknown. I stayed for another two weeks and then was officially released. I had to report, I told my wife, to a demob centre in Surrey somewhere. I was given a railway warrant and discharge papers and a date to go.

The day soon arrived. I kissed my wife and caught my train to Fenchurch Street, Waterloo and Surrey. I took a bus to the demob centre, and arrived with a sort of apprehensive feeling. But it was like a conveyor belt, as I stood in line, and then went through the system of changing my uniform for an ill fitting striped navy blue suit and hat, and it all seemed to be over in no time. Now I was just a guy looking for work. So back I went to my Richmond Avenue home to my wife, who was not pregnant, in Shoeburyness. My army pay would soon come to an end and my wife would soon have to leave her work. So we would need somewhere else to live shortly.

Well, my letter came for me to attend a police training course with the Met at Imber Court in a few weeks time. So, in my new demob suit, I went to London, and eventually to the police school at Imber Court, where I was soon made very welcome. I was shown where I would sleep and eat and told some of the rules to obey while I was there. My course started the next morning with a visit to the school classroom, where a teacher was spelling out what we would be doing for the next four weeks. As I listened, I began to feel quite excited. I remember we were then driven in a van to the Tower of London, and we wee escorted to where the crown jewels were in a large glass rotunda. They were beautiful to see. As I gazed at them, we were being told how the Metropolitan police protected them, which they promised they would show us at the next place we would call at that day, Scotland Yard, headquarters of the Met. We were welcomed there by a senior police officer and shown the fingerprint department and all that went with it. Then came the forensic department, and we were a very long time there having it all explained to us, including homicide. Then we saw the protection device for the crown jewels. Well, I couldn't believe it! It was a receiver from the Tower of London to a device which would start a gramophone record playing in this room in Scotland Yard saying, "There is an intruder". And that was all that was to it!

Well, that was one of the most interesting day, and there were plenty more to come. I was eager to see what would happen the next day. The evenings were very pleasant, and there was a bar and restaurant and cafes. There were sports in the grounds that we could join in with between classes and homework. There was a driving school, where my brother had spent time, on becoming a driver in the Kingston Metropolitan police. Some of the instructors they remembered him, which was good. He had joined the Met, long before when he was demobbed from the Scots Guards. I suppose this was why I wanted to be in the police.

Anyway, the next day, we went around all the courts in London and attended the trials of the Old Bailey. This was a murder trial. And of course, we went to the civil courts, where crimes of theft or even prostitution were tied. After many cases had been head the very last case was always the parade of the London prostitutes. They would simply file past the judge, who would find them equally; I think it was something like five shilling each. This was customary. We spent all day doing these trials and writing notes, having breaks, and lunch as well. So the time seemed to fly by. Then it was back to good old Imber Court, homework and relaxing in the bar, with darts or snooker. There was plenty to do here, every evening, so no complaints.

I think the day after that was the one of the mock trials, where we had to be either the judge or the jury or a prisoner or solicitor, playing out the scenes from our visits to the courts the day before. It was good fun as well as being helpful, if we ever became policeman. Then there were visits to the police Horse training centres and the dog training centres. There were police films in the Cinema there. One we had to watch was "The Blue Lamp" with Jack Warner, and I was told he sometimes came there himself on a visit.

I think the best part of the course was when we went with the Thames River police and were told all about what they did as we spent all day on the river in the police launch. They would talk about the bodies. They had to take out of the river and the suicides, "bridge jumpers", they called them. Then there were times we had to escort the pilots on to the big ships and go aboard ourselves. It was very interesting, all this river work. I could fill a book with all the interesting things we did on the police course, all paid for by the army, but all good things come to an end, and we were soon saying goodbye to our instructors and the friends we had made.

It was now time to go back home to my dear wife, who had moved in to live with her mother, who had been rehoused on a brand-new estate halfway between Shoeburyness and Southend. We were soon to have our first child, a boy. We named him Kenneth

Alfred. He was a lovely boy. I soon got a letter to go to Whitehall to see if I had passed my police course. I attended the Whitehall rooms opposite the Cenotaph, and there seemed to be hundreds of would-be policemen there, all over 6 foot, with no beards and all very smart in their demob suits or other suits. I think I wore my wedding suit. I know I was very smart and over six foot tall.

We were ushered into a big hall and told the rules. "You will have a medical. You will be assessed on your interests. You will be asked all sorts of things about what you have done or whether you have been in trouble with the police in the past. You will be asked what books you read, but what you will not be told is why you failed. If you fail. You will simply be told you have failed and given your return money home." So, then off we went on our conveyor belt. First, the medical: eyes, ears, legs, bend down, any piles? Breath test, height measurement's, weight, teeth, arms and legs, feet, everything was thoroughly examined. Then into the interrogation room we went.

"What hobbies do you have? What religion are you? Do you attend church on a regular basis? What sports are you into? Are you single or married? How do you get on? What books do you read?" The questioning was endless. We walked through to another room, where we answered more questions, and then back to the big hall." Sit quiet," we were told. "You will have your name read out if you have failed." So you sit through loads of names being read out, hoping that yours won't be. But then there it is, "Alfred Wynne", and you join the other might-have-beens living up for their fare home.

Then it's back to Waterloo, then Fenchurch Street, then home to Shoeburyness, and pack a few things remaining, and go on to the new address on the new Whittingham Estate, and your lovely wife and beautiful son. But then came my daughter, and we had to start looking for different accommodation for our growing family. But while I was at Shoeburyness, I had begun work on a brickfield as a labourer. Having failed to become a policeman, I needed a better job than pushing a wheelbarrow full of bricks.

Then one day I heard a man shouting on the railway, which ran alongside the brickfield. I went over and found there were some boys or young men larking about being shouted at by this man in a suit and bowler hat, laying down the law in pure Liverpool language, i.e. Scouse. So through the fence I called him over and we chatted about

Liverpool and the army and my efforts to join the police. It seemed he was the foreman of the railway yard of the Shoeburyness railway. I asked if they needed any more men. He told me to write to Euston station to a person he gave me the details of.

My foreman of the brickfield came over and told me in no uncertain manner to get back to work. Well, I wrote to Euston the very next day, and waited for a reply. It soon became and invited me to attend Euston for an evaluation test. They gave me the full address and time and date, and I went to the evaluation test. This was a brief medical, a thorough eyes and ears test, and then some questions to be answered. They told me they would be in touch, and that was that, I thought. But a few days later, they gave me a time and date to start work as an engine cleaner at Shoeburyness Depot. I was over the moon to think I could leave the brickworks and work on the other side of the fence. They said I would be attending a railway school in London some days, but it wouldn't cost me as I now had a railway pass to go anywhere free.

Working for the Railway

So my new working life began in the early hours of the morning, when it was very quiet at Shoeburyness except for the hissing of the steam coming from some of the engines waiting to be lit and fired up ready for the driver and fireman to come. In the meantime, I had to trim the lamps and start the fires in the fireboxes and set the lamps as well, and clean the engines with cotton waste and diesel. I loved my new job, even though I had to ride my bike from the new estate to Shoeburyness railway depot in the early hours in all sorts of weather, as it was wintertime when I joined. But I got on well, right from the start, with some of the old boys and drivers and firemen and cleaners like me, and, of course, Mr. Harper, my foreman with the bowler hat. He never took it off.

Well, you had to do so many cleaning jobs to become a passed cleaner. If a fireman was short, a passed cleaner could take his place. Of course, if you are a passed cleaner, you h ad to know the rules of the road, the road being the railway track. Then as a passed cleaner, you started to have fireman duties, and when you had done so many of these, you became a fireman. I found by turning up for someone who was off sick. I was able to progress much quicker than all the others. And as the summer approached, I soon became a fireman. Then it was worth all the cleaning jobs I had done. I felt like a driver, since the driver would let you take over sometimes, and it felt good.

There was money to be made, also, out on the road. Our main road was from Shoeburyness to Fenchurch Street and Fenchurch to Tilbury. That was where you could do well, at Tilbury, while you wee there, quite close to the liners docking and all those rich people coming to our lovely country for their holidays. All I had to do was change my hat from a fireman's hat to a porter's hat and grab a barrow and say, "Porter, Sir", and I was in for some very nice tips! Then there were the weddings. The best man would tip you to blow the whistle a few times as you left the station and all the travelling you did in the carriage was paid for by the railway. So, all in all, it was very good.

But at home, it was hard, trying to find a room or a house for my family. You couldn't get a council house. You were on a very long list. People were jumping the queue by obtaining points more than you by illness or other reasons. So it was very hard for me, and especially for my Betty. We looked for rooms. At one time we had the offer to look after a widower and his two sons, in return for living with them in his small house. My Betty had washing and cooking and tidying to do for them, and her own family to look after. We now had three children, another baby boy to go with Kenneth and Valerie. The house wasn't too far from a railway bridge, where I would be on the engine to wave to them as I went under the railway bridge on my way to Tilbury or Fenchurch Street. The children loved it, my Betty would tell me when I got home. But our accommodation was terrible. We were constantly on the move in all kinds of weather, pushing a pram with all we had in the world on our backs, or a pushchair.

We actually lived in another place in Warrior Square, Southend-on-Sea, where the people living above us would have to bring their rubbish out via our living room. And I think upstairs was a brothel. We didn't have a great start for our married life. But we both tried hard in our different ways. Then one day, we heard from Betty's mum that we had finally got a house to call our own from Southend Council. It was a prefab, 136 Rochford Road, Southend-on-Sea, and it was lovely. My wife was very house-proud and everything shone, the floors, the curtains, everything was like a palace.

I had to take my boots or shoes off before I was allowed through the door, but she did keep the place nice. The prefab was pure luxury. It had a built-in fridge and a washing machine. All the rooms were square, so it was easy to decorate. It was all on the same level and very big. We really did enjoy most of the time we lived there. But then gradually, things began to go wrong. I would come home to an empty house, and no dinner. She had taken herself off to her mother's. This happened much too frequently. We began to have rows about it and then she would prevent me from entering her bedroom. I then had very had pains in my chest and had to attend the chest clinic, where the doctor told me I was in the wrong job with my past medical record. He was referring to my TB, and the pleurisy and pneumonia

I had suffered in the past. The smoke from the steam engines was not helping my scarred lungs, he said, and he ordered me to lave my railway job. This didn't help matters at home, and I now had to find more work.

This I did. I was still employed, and how this came about was that when I was doing temporary postman work at Christmas, I would deliver Christmas mail and empty the post boxes and then sort mail at the Southend sorting office. While I was there, I got to know some people, who had been there for years. I asked them about joining the Post office and they said that if they had their time again they would join the telephone section. So I wrote away and applied. I was given a job on the Southend-on-Sea Post Office telephones. We installed phones, or rather, at first I assisted in installing them. We collected telegraph poles, dressed them and planted them. Then, after a while, I was sent on a course to Bletchley, where I would become a telephone engineer.

Now I could install telephones with my assistant. I was called an engineer class 2B. I soon got some good and some bad jobs to do, but on the whole I was quite satisfied with what I had achieved after having to give up the railway job. I can remember stringing cables, crossing the main road with the traffic underneath me, to the Southend swimming pool. I had to lift my dangling feet as I sat in a sort of bo'sun's chair high above the road, and we had to climb telegraph poles with our leg-iron spikes, and at the top repair or replace units.

Things were still going from bad to worse, as my wife informed me she was thinking of a separation. This didn't help matters at all. She said she now had a solicitor, and she was going ahead. I used to see her coming home, wiping her make-up off as she came home, and she was now getting all our neighbours on her side. So I would find her not at home or in her friend's house, across the road. I saw her go there one night of many nights. I went to her friend's house and through the letterbox I saw her and her friend trying to abort a baby. I didn't even know she was pregnant. I thought after witnessing this act that this baby was not mine. And soon after she left me and started divorce proceedings against me. I was forced out of my home, which she soon came back to with her children and her baby son Simon. Before Simon there was Keith. So now there were three boys and a girl. And as I know now, all four were mine.

Proceedings for Divorce

But to go back to the story of my life, I took lodgings in Southend and tried to get on with my life, still trying without success to see my children. I lost my job at the Post Office. I then went to work with the oil refinery at Corytown, Shell Haven, as it was called. I used to get a bus, supplied by Shell, to work from Southend and back again. Each time I arrived home there was another letter from her solicitor, and eventually one sending a summons for me to attend the law courts in London for a divorce hearing. So all this I had to do alone.

As a result of being the breadwinner of the family, I was ordered to pay for the children and her, my ex, an amount of hard earned cash. I was at my wits end. I joined the International Friendship League in Southend, to keep my sanity, and had some nice friends there. One friend was a floorwalker in Keddies, a big department store at Victoria Circus, southend. He lived in Southchurch, and told me his friend was a medium, a spiritualist of some kind, and he would like me to meet him at have a reading from him, which might help me in my present situation. This I agreed to do. Then one day, in Keddies, my friend told me that his friend would be home from sea, the Saturday coming and it would be a good time for me to see him for my reading. So I look forward to the time I would spend in his beautiful house, after my lousy digs.

I rang the bell on this Saturday at my friend's door, and waited a little nervously. Then my friend opened his front door. "Hello, Alfred, come in." There was a tape recording playing as I entered his lounge. It was a recording of a séance he had had there some time ago, he explained, and went to switch it off." No," I said, "I should like to hear it. It sounds very interesting." What I could hear were questions being asked and a voice, very calmly giving precise answers. The questions were like, "What is light?" And the answer coming back, you had to believe. They all made sense. It was marvellous. I was dumbfounded. It was very quiet and nice and cosy sitting there, listening and enjoying this tape recording, with a nice cup of tea and cakes. I felt very relaxed there, I must say.

Then the doorbell rang and in came my friend's friend, the medium. He sat down and we were introduced. We chatted about the weather, the political situation, the ships at sea, and just enjoy each other's company. Then, as we get some more sandwiches and had more cups of tea, the time came for my reading. I was ushered into another nice room and asked to sit on one of the nice chairs there. My friend went out of the room, shutting the door behind him, leaving me, and his friend in the room. I'll call his friend Tom. He said, "Excuse me for a moment", and he sat, putting his hands across his face, and bowing his head. It was only a moment. Then he sat up and I said, "Do you need anything of mine?" He replied that he didn't, adding, "I'm not into that nonsense". Then, he said, "Let's just be very quiet and still for a few moments while I gather myself."

So I obliged. Then he said, "Well, who would you want to contact if you could?"

"My dear mother," I said.

"Well," he said, let's see what happens."

The lights were on brightly in the room. There were no mystic objects or pictures, anywhere. He spoke.

"I see a room, pretty dark, although it's not nighttime. I see a piano with something on top of it. I can't make it out. I think it's a gramophone on top of the piano. It was a big horn. Now a sideboard with a stuffed animal in a glass case, and there are two concrete steps down to a small scullery. The curtains have tassels on them. There is nobody in the room. The room is not very big. There is something else. It's like a small shrine over a bed. The bed is in the room. I think that's it for now, Alfred."

"Well, how did we do?" he asked eventually. "Was it to do with your mother?"

"No," I said, "but you have just described my grandmother's room, exactly."

Well, thinking about what he had told me, I thought it was amazing. How could he know these things? And although he hadn't mentioned anything about my mother, my mother did live there once.

"Well, what job have you got now, Alfred?" I said that I was at the oil refinery. He said, "Let's see." Then he said, "Do you like it there?" I said that I did. He said, "Well, you won't be there soon. I can see you in a large place, a big enclosure. It's a factory or something like that and there's a strong smell of paint, and a lot of noise. A lot of noise. There's a lot of hammering and shouting and singing. There's a lot going on there, Alfred."

I said, or I think I said, "Why should I leave my job? I've no intention of leaving my job." So we went back into the nice lounge again, and to my surprise, his friend was putting his coat on and saying his goodbyes. Then he was gone.

"How did it go, Alfred?" my friend said. I told him what had happened, and he said, "Sometimes he gets it wrong." I said, "Oh no, it wasn't wrong. He described my grandmother's home, and I thought it was marvellous." I said, "He didn't charge me anything." "No, that's right, he doesn't."

All the way back to my digs, I was going over and over in my mind what had happened, asking myself how he could have known these things. It was then that I thought I would go and see my ex and the children, and see if we could start again. She invited me in and gave me something to eat, and them, in no uncertain manner, told me to go or she would call the police. So off I went again. I took myself to the pictures and halfway through the film I couldn't breathe without pain. So I gingerly crept back up the aisle and out of the cinema.

I was walking, in a lot of pain, along Southend High Street. I felt in such pain I stopped for a while, and realised I was leaning on a brass plate that said, "Doctor Something" on it. I rang the bell and the doctor himself came to the door.

"What do you want?" he said. "I'm closed, and I don't know what the hell you're doing here. I don't know you."

I managed to tell him I was in a lot of pain. Eventually, he said, "I think you'd better come in."

He led me into his surgery, and I asked him, "Can someone get a spontaneous pneumothorax, a collapsed lung, by doing nothing?"

"You think that is what is wrong with you?" I just about nodded. "Well, my man, I think you're right. You must walk very slowly and get yourself home and rest. See your own doctor as soon as you can. Have you had this before?"

"No," I said. "I was a male nurse once."

"Well, just do what I say, walk home, very slowly, and then rest."

So I rested for few days, and it cured itself. But before it did, I had an abscess on my tooth, while I still had the pneumothorax. I went to our dentist in the High Street and asked for gas instead of an injection. He must have phoned my wife because he came back to me, still in the chair and said, "Are you trying to get me locked up? You asked me for gas. I was about to give it to you. And if I had, you would not be dead. You only have one lung at the moment. You won't be having gas."

I thought, "Someone still loves me a little bit." So I had the injection, not gas.

Well, I didn't give up on a reconciliation with my Betty and decided to try again. I gave her all the money I had and she said, perhaps we could give it a go. So I thought, having lost yet another job, I would try and get some work again/. There were some ways I could try. There was an aerodrome just up the road from the prefab. So I went there to see if I could get a job.

The aerodrome was KLM, and a man called Mr. Keegan, who I had been told in the past was the person the K stood for, was on the premises. He gave me an interview in his office. I poured out my sad story to him. At the end, he said, "Would you take any job?" I said that I would. He told me I could start right away, cleaning the outside of aircraft, with Duraglit. A huge tin was given to me, so I got started. It was easy enough, and it was money that I needed. While I was cleaning and polishing, Mr. K came up to me and asked, "How are you getting on?"

"Okay," I said. "Well," he said, "if you would like to work overtime, I could let you do that, and it might help both of us."

"Yes." I jumped at his offer but said, "If I'm working late, I'll need sandwiches. If I could pop home and get some, it would help."

"Yes, all right. Go now, and good luck." Off I went for my sandwiches. I was sure she would do this for me if I had a job. As I approached the prefab, I could see a large furniture van outside. Loading our furniture into it were two men. My father-in-law was there holding the baby and my wife was standing there with the other children. My heart sank. I cried as I chased the departing van and my family. The door to the prefab was still open.

It was getting late now, very dark. I went into the empty prefab. There was nothing left. I pulled out some metal drawers, laid them together on the floor, and started to lie down on them to go to sleep. I couldn't sleep so I got up and went out into the street. I was devastated. I had no money, no family, nothing.

I just walked and walked. I found myself on Southend Pier, looking at the water. I just wanted to die, and the next thing I remember was something grabbing hold of me. In a little while, the something spoke.

Surely you have someone you can go to, my brother lives in Kingston Surrey but I have nothing no money at all to get there then I felt my hand being grabbed well you have now this voice said and just like a shadow was gone. I found myself in Southend central railway station clutching a ten pound note as I sat in a railway carriage I didn't know what was happening to me as the train gathered speed I gradually began to recall where I was and where I was going and why then I must have drifted to sleep the next thing I remember is some one shaking me and yelling Fenchurch Street come on your here well it was underground train next to Waterloo then the train to Kingston then a bus the 65 to Richmond then my stop in Tudor Drive then a small walk to Barnfield gdns No 25 and I was at my brothers home ringing the doorbell, my brothers wife opened the door then shouted its Alfie to her husband as she ushered me into the living room where I flopped down on the settee I'll put the kettle on she said as she went off to the kitchen leaving my brother and I alone to talk My brother said the Southend police have been on to me they thought you were dead it seems they looked in your window of the prefab and saw the two metal draws they thought it was a body until they broke in. Anyway Alf what I propose is this I know a fella who has a lorry I'll see him in the morning and ask him if I can borrow it for the day and we can go to Southend and see if they have left any furniture and bring it here Ok so for now Alf drink your tea and Gladys will show you to your room goodnight son and off I went to bed because it was now very late.

True to his word, my brother had borrowed a lorry for the day. He said, "Are you ready?"?? Southend, we went, just my brother and I. There was nothing left there in the prefab except a wardrobe and my piano, so having loaded what he decided to take, we made our journey back to Kingston. I was close to tears all the way, until something happened as we were nearly back at his house. We were approaching a group of shops on our left, my brother's local shops. There was a lorry outside the shops and a man on top sorting out his load, but between this man's lorry and ours, there was a bigger lorry driving in front of us. The man who was sorting out his load fell and the lorry in front of our others ran over him. It tipped once and then twice, as first the front wheels went over him and then the rear wheels. All my troubles left me as my brother ran into the shop to phone for help and an ambulance. I threw my coat over the man and stayed to give him what comfort I could. As time went by, we learnt, the man was not too badly hurt. It seemed wheels went over his hips as he lay on his side. My prayers had been answered for this man, I believe, and my troubles seemed less important. It is strange what happens in life.

Well, the next thing was work. My brother's house was a police house, so it was subsidised by the Metropolitan police, but I still had to give him money for I keep. My brother had said I had to live with him, because my first wife divorced me in the London law courts, on the grounds of mental cruelty. In those days, the breadwinner always had to pay to keep people to save the state having to pay. I was ordered to pay maintenance for my four children and for my wife. I had to give my brother money for my keep, and as I never earned much in those days, I took on three or four jobs, working a 24 hour day.

My first job was in a sheet metal engineering place where I worked from 8 a.m. to 5 p.m. My next job was from 6 p.m. to 9 p.m. My third job was from 10 p.m. to 6 a.m. My first job consisted of cutting and bending sheet metal. My next job, the hardest, was in the Kingston Power Station (coal-fired). The job entailed cleaning clinker from the fire grates that were put out to be cleaned. This would be tackled by a group of strong young men of whom I was one. We had to rig a huge block and tackle holding the grate of the coaling furnace, the grate being horizontal on the bottom of the furnace. We would attach a hook to one end of the grate, and pull—hoist it up, until it was vertical. Then, with large iron crowbars, we would to knock the clinker off the grate.

Of course, between these jobs, I would nip home for a quick nap and food and clean clothes. My last job was all night, starting at 10 p.m. This entailed dry-cleaning all of the London shows' costumes. A van would wait until all the shows had finished the evening performance, then go around and gather all the costumes to be dry cleaned by me and others. I've had some of the costumes on, myself, like Flanagan and Allen's big fur coat and hat, and turbans from Kismet. When we had finished, the costumes, about 3 AM, we would then dry-clean sheepskins until morning. This was bonus work. These were my three occupations to earn money to send to my ex-wife and children and to pay my brother.

Then my brother told me I had to leave his house, because the Metropolitan police had found out that he had me living there. So the day he told me I thought I would ask the Kingston on Thames YMCA if they could offer me accommodation, as I had nowhere to live from that day on. The secretary said he was very sorry, but that the Kingston YMCA were not equipped to take people in to board, and that the nearest YMCA that was was in Wimbledon. So that evening I went to the YMCA in Wimbledon, add was welcomed by a very nice secretary, who had been informed from Kingston. He said, "We have been expecting you. You are very welcome. Your evening meal awaits you once we have shown you your room." I felt very relieved and was soon introduced to my two roommates. Then, I enjoyed a lovely meal in the dining room, where I was introduced to the longest resident in the YMCA. He was nicknamed Tiny, because of his huge size, both tall and broad, and with a full Royal Navy beard, but he was a gentle man. He wore the uniform of a navy steward. My two roommates were Nigel and David. David was soon my very best friend. He was a Cambridge eight, and we hit it off right away. We talked about his university life, politics, and the stars and planets well into my first night there, while Nigel slept.

My first priority was to find a job, as it was Christmas, and Christmas in those days meant, as far as employment was concerned, that the last man to join a firm was always dismissed at Christmas. This was something to do with running a business in those days. Anyway, the next day I went looking for work. I tried several places around Wimbledon and finished up in New Malden. I tried some more there and finally came to the Decca record company, where the records were made. And here I was very successful. I was given a job making gramophone records. I was show how they were made with a tour of the factory and in three days I was making the records of songs, bands and singers. They were all the records I might have bought as well. Then there were famous recording artists will very often visited, and I could see them all from my machine.

Well, having settled into my new home and sorted my means of paying for my accommodation I began to enjoy Wimbledon itself. Opposite to the YMCA there was the Wimbledon Theatre. This was the Broadway Wimbledon, the name of the high street there, and one end was Wimbledon Common. There was a cinema down the other end, and there was a Presbyterian Church or Kirk, with the Rev. Black in charge, who would preach a wonderful sermon. David had got me interested in his church. I soon met some wonderful people in the congregation. I went regularly, and as it was Christmas took part in the carol singing as well as other activities. We went carol singing with the girl's college, and then we organised a skiffle group. I was the one on the tea chest. These friends were wonderful. One man and his wife, whom we became very good friends with, was Dr. Donald Mackay. He had something to do with the invention of radar for the war. He was a physicist. We often h ad dinner at his house in Wimbledon, and sometimes a musical evening when a group of young boys and girls would listen to and discuss recordings of music by Borodin or Rimsky Korsakov, music like Scheherazade or Polovtsian Dances.

They were very nice times for me, however, my wife and children were always somewhere in my mind. I used to travel to see my children at least once every week. I took the train to Waterloo station, then the tube to Fenchurch Street station, then got off at Southend-on-Sea Central Station, then took a bus to Whittingham, South Church, Southend-on-Sea. My children would be accompanied by a complete stranger and handed over to me in a field near where their mother lived, but I never saw her. I would take the four children out to Peter Pan's playground, spoil them a little bit, then take them back to the field, and then make the long journey back to Wimbledon. This got into quite a routine as time went on. The place where I would meet my children changed, because that was her parents' house, so she moved back into our prefab at 136 Rochford Road.

Then one day, I was really worried about how she was coping, because they had a violent snowstorm in Essex and Tiny said, "If you're all that worried, I'll drive you to Southend in my car". And that's what happened. The snow was awful on the roads to Southend. I didn't think we would make it, but eventually we got there. I felt terrible, because when we arrived we were greeted by the sounds of a party going on. She was not having a party but had her friends there from across the road. She told me to go, and her friends pushed me out of the door. So in the end, I said to Tiny. "It's no good. She won't talk to me". I was hoping I could as I had done before, have a reconciliation with my wife. But as I say she was not interested. So Tiny drove me back to Wimbledon YMCA. It was then that I gave up on any hope of reconciliation and began to make a new life for myself.

Making a New Life for Myself

I started to learn old-time dancing at the Coronation Hall in Kingston on Thames, and met several ladies. One, Muriel, was a very good dancer and wanted me for a partner, and after a while together, we were getting very good marks and going to Brighton and places to dance with other groups. I was getting too fond of Muriel, because she didn't tell me she was married. So it was time to lave my Viennese Waltz and find pastures new. My next girlfriend was another Betty. She had been left with a baby boy by a sailor. The boy was two years old now, and she lived with her mother in New Malden, but she had a stop of her own, with staff. She was a very good hairdresser, and she was very good to me. I had to go to hospital and she was the only one to come and visit me in Kingston Hospital. Then there was Doreen, a red haired Welsh girl, but I spoke to that one night, and that was that.

I was living it up, but it wasn't the same. I did contemplate marriage with my Betty hairdresser, but after talking it over with my brother Fred, he talked me out of it. So I continued with my life in the YMCA. I met another girl when I went ballroom dancing at the Coronation Hall in Kingston on Thames, one evening. I couldn't believe my eyes when I saw this girl and a girlfriend, looking everyone over. It was my ex-wife looking for me. I saw her first and steered my partner towards the exit. As I left with my briefly new girlfriend, I thought, "No chance!" My ex-wife had hurt me so very deeply that now there was no way back. She had had her chance several times but didn't want me back. I was now over the hurt and didn't want anymore from her.

As time went on, my friends I had come to know and lover were leaving the YMCA. There was one chap who was a working to leave the country. He was at work in Wimbledon's Woolworths for every minute of everyday to make enough money to pay his way to emigrate to Alberta in Canada. He had a plan for his life, and he knew the exact date, after a while, of when he was leaving. He kept himself very much to himself. But we all loved the guy and admired the way he had planned all trip out. We told him it would be very cold out there. He said, "Yes, but that is secondary to my trip or voyage". So we all chipped in for a going away present for him. We bought him a Bible and lots of warm clothes.

While I was living with my brother and his family in 25 Bonfield Gardens, off Tudor Drive, Kingston on Thames, apart from working in the engineering and in the power station and in the dry cleaning factory, and not forgetting I also worked in the Kingston hotel and a garage, I saw an advertisement for a fitter's mate. Well, I had done this in the engineers', so I went to see about this job. This was in Teddington, must on the borders of Kingston and a stone's throw from Hampton Court Palace. It was just a small shop when I got there, and an elderly gentleman said, "This vacancy is for an electrician's mate, not a fitter's mate. Sorry, son, have you come far?" I said, "Not too far, but I have no job at the moment and I have always been interested in electrical work. I am very keen to work at it."

"All right, son, I'll give you a trial and if you pass it, you're in."

Well, this was the beginning of my eventual occupation as an electrician. My first job was in Woolworths shop in Enfield, and I had to travel alone on a train to meet up with the electricity at the Enfield shop. As the train got to the Enfield station, it was a dead end stop. The train didn't go further any further. As I was walking towards the gate at the end of the platform, a man came to my side and put a 10 bob note in my hand. He said, "Please look straight ahead, Sir. You're in a film." I never knew what film it was, but somewhere I'm in a film.

I found my way to the High Street in Enfield, and the Woolworths shop, which was newly built. I also found my electrician, a big Irishman with red hair. He was a pleasant chap, and soon brought me to work. I enjoyed it; all the girls eyeing me was a bonus. I did eventually date one before the job there was finished. Sometimes I would have to go out to our wholesalers in south London. I went quite often, and was getting to know London quite well. The next big job I had was in a new Woolworths in Brighton. This job was a long job. So we would have to live there for a while. I didn't mind that at all. As I packed my best clothes and shoes, ties etc, I plan to see something of the night life, and the icing on the cake for me was that we would travel each weekend from London, on the Brighton Belle, with all its luxury, all paid for by the firm. We also had our digs arranged for us by the firm. Mine was a lovely boardinghouse with a very pleasant landlady in Worthing. This was my home for a few weeks, all as long as the job took. My electrician was Tom, my redheaded mate, and we had some great nights together. Also, I was amazed to see a huge department store, Bentall's. This was the second of these out of the world stores I had seen. The first one was in Kingston on Thames.

We were allowed home at weekends, if we hadn't been asked to work overtime, and if we wanted to go, so it was a very good job I had landed myself. When the Brighton job came to an end the next job—well, I couldn't believe it—was the Woolworths in Southend-on-Sea. I thought I would be able to see more of my children, and it was going to be another long job. We had to build them an escalator. The digs were arranged and Ginger and I set off for Fenchurch Street, then Southend Central. I didn't need any maps. I found it hadn't changed much.

Once I was settled in my digs in York Road I explored. The Kursaal was still going strong, and all the nightlife was much the same. I renewed my friendships, and sometimes I found myself looking to see if I could see "you know who". However, I did see someone I knew, my sister Freda. She was working in the Woolworths said I was to work in. It seems she was friends with my ex-wife and was living with her. That was a surprise! I told my sister not to tell Betty I was in Southend. I honestly did not want her at all. That part of my life was in the past. She had hurt me enough.

Well, the job went very well, and soon Woolworths of Southend-on-Sea was boasting a brand-new escalator, and we were moving on. I had met an electrician, who was working for a contractor called Rashleigh Phipps, and he was telling me about all the money he was getting, and all the perks and good digs. Taking everything into account, I could be earning a lot more with this other electrical contractor. So I made a decision to move jobs once more. My ex-wife was bleeding me drive through her solicitors. Well, I got my new job right away. They were installing very high lights over the Upminster underground railway terminus yards. It meant I would be paid danger money for working so high, but it paid well and I had good digs.

In Upminster itself not far from the job that suited me I found my own digs and I was just part of a nice little family, the lady of the house spoilt me and the kids loved me and it made me feel right at home. My work continued until the contract ran out at Upminster so once more I transferred to another job a firm of electrical contractors called Troughton and Young and this firm were working on a new extension to the Ford Motor Co at Dagenham east London So I needed to find more lodgings and these were to be in the Town of Romford in eastern ave. I soon settled in my new home It was good there even Though I had to share my room with another lodger, but he seemed a nice sort a student And we soon got on well, and the landlady was very nice too. I soon settled in to my new Abode so one evening I decided that I would explore my new town at the end of my avenue was the Romford high street and across the road opposite me was a dance hall with some lovely music coming from it I could see people dancing as I looked up at the first floor windows. As I loved to dance this I couldn't pass up so across the road I went And was soon at the kiosk where you pay to go in then up the stairs to the dancehall I think I looked quite smart and as I stood there on the edge of the dance floor across the other side I noticed a girl looking so sad and lonely I felt sorry to see her like that I thought if no one asks her to dance the next one then I will ask here, well the usual applause rang out as the band finished playing the foxtrot and the couples made there Way back to their tables where they were camped for the evening no one approached the girl so it was my turn now I walked across the floor toward her and then as I did a couple Joined her but I was so close to her that I asked her if I could have the next dance she hesitated then her friends go on go she said yes I would love to then the band began playing again this time a waltz and off we went gliding across the floor it felt good dancing with her, she was a very good dancer and she looked more beautiful the more I looked at her and she was now smiling and looking like she was enjoying every moment on the dance she wasn't that sad girl that I saw across the floor when I first came in and I thought if I had anything to do with this transformation then I was very pleased as we danced I asked her name Cynthia she was What a lovely name I thought then do you live here in Romford oh no she said I live in Grays in Thurrock this meant nothing to me I had never heard of the place and do you work here no she said I work in an office in the city what city I saw the city of London she replied are you a typist then well sort of she said I am shorthand typist and a secretary. Oh I'm sorry I she cut me off don't worry I understand she said, and what do you do me oh I am an electrician as the waltz finished I asked her if she would like a coffee or something coffee is fine she said so off I went to join the que when I returned with the drinks she wasn't there I had left her, then I saw her with her two friends waving to me to join them they had a table and also a chair for me with the next dance her friends "Irene and Bob" went for the next dance leaving Cynthia and I to sit and chat. Cynthia told me she lived with her mother and did all the housework when she gets home from work each evening and that she two sisters and five brothers all married except her and one brother who also lived with mother soon her friends joined us again so that put an end to our chat so we went back to our dancing again but the time with Cynthia just flew by and it wasn't long before we were dancing the last waltz together it had been a wonderful evening for me I think no I know I fell in love with Cynthia. Well we were soon at the cloakroom retrieving our topcoats to leave.

The dance hall and go our separate ways outside we said our good byes to Cynthia' friends then I asked Cynthia if she would like another coffee goodness no she said I have to hurry or I will miss my last bus so she was soon running across the road To her bus stop opposite the dance hall and me trying to keep up with her we joined the Que for the bus and suddenly it was here and Cynthia was soon stepping on to the platform. I shouted Cynthia `` and a lot of heads turned" What is your phone Number As she shouted it back I quickly scribbled it on the back of my left hand and as the bus left I could only hope that I had taken the number correctly. My Cynthia had gone and I felt all alone again,

I prayed as I saw the bus depart, that I had taken the phone number down on my hand correctly then I hurried back to my lodgings I flopped down on my bed and lay on my Back thinking about Cynthia. It had been a long time since I had felt so much emotion About a girl I had only just met. The bus must be given time to get to Cynthia's Destination so all I could do for now was wait I

kept looking at my wrist watch on my Table at the side of my bed I
gave it half an hour and then asked the land lady if I could use her
phone she took me into the hall and pointed to a pay phone I thanked
her and she departed I looked at the number that I had trasferd into
my note book took a deep breath and started to dial Hello came a
stern voice hello who is this I replyed is Cynthia There no she wont
be here for some time she has gone to a dance in Romford tonight
oh I said would you tell her Alfred had phoned and will ring back. I
sank back on my bed and I must have drifted off for a few minutes
because my watch told me so I jumped quickly off my bed and was
soon back on the phone. Hello is that Cynthia we were soon Back
in conversation again we talked at some length about our evening I
then asked if I could see her again she sounded pleased as she said
yes I would like that but it wouldn't be until the next Saturday that
suited me fine as I needed to settle in both my new abode and my
new place of work, and as long as we were going to meet again then I
could easily wait until Saturday. I worked twice as hard all that week
to make the time go so as Saturday would come much quicker and
I could soon be with Cynthia again I could not stop talking about
her to my Pals at work. One of my pals had a motor bike and he also
lived in Romford he offered to take me back to my lodging each day
after work on the back of his bike this was great as when Saturday
eventually Arrived I was soon whisked back to Romford and showered
and dressed, I could hardly eat my evening meal with the excitement
I was feeling at the thought I would soon be on my prearranged date
with my Cynthia, as my heart told me she was. I soon found my self
nervy standing at the bus stop outside the dance hall, opposite the
one that I had last seen Cynthia leaving me last Saturday, but that was
history now I told my self And soon I saw the "370" bus approach
The bus stop I stood back to let the people on the bus get off then
there she was, and she looked lovely as the sun cought her fair hair
and she smiled as she said well here I am Alfred I remember I said and
you look lovely. So off we went along Romford road with all its shops
and people scurrying along Would you like a coffee or something I
found it hard to find words to say I was so excited inside. Anyway I
was soon my old talkative self as we sat with our drinks and waited
for our toasted tea cakes that I had orderd She said so you work at
Fords Dagenham yes I said then she said my train go's past there every

morning and we that is my girl friends and I often wave to the boys working there as we go by just for a giggle she added, perhaps I could see you one morning. I will do my best to see you I said what time she said about 8:40. O.K. Who did I speak to on the phone oh she said that was my mother I said how far away do you live well a fair way she said we soon ate our tea cakes and paid up and left. Outside the sun was still shining as she put her arm in mine we talked to each other about things in general and then she told me she had just come back from Canada She had gone with her best friend she added that one of her older sisters lived there in Winnipeg I said that was handy somewhere to stay oh no she said we only stayed one night there When we arrived as she explained it was a working holiday they her friend and her had arranged employment with a firm of solicitors out there who had officers all over Canada so the idea was for the two of them to travel all over Canada and she said her boss and the firm she worked for here gave her their blessing.

And that her and her friend had a great time on the "Empress of Britain" going out to Canada and gradually the truth behind the trip came out and she told me that she had been jilted at the alter and had suffered a break down in her health as a result her boss here had given her time to heal by suggesting this working holiday to get over it all he didn't want to loose his talented secretary and the whole shipping office where she worked wished her "Bon Voyage" as she opened up all these things to me it made me love her even more, after all I had a few things to confess myself But not just yet as the day wore on I suggested lunch we found a nice restaurant I was wondering about how much it was going to cost me when Cynthia said don't worry have what you like we can use my luncheon vouchers what had left me short of cash was maintenance for four children and an undeserving ex wife but I wasn't ready to tell Cynthia about all that not just yet

I was very happy now with my new girl friend so now just wasn't the time there would be other times to tell her about my four children and my divorce at the moment though I was just sitting here enjoying my lovely company and a very nice meal. As usual the time seemed to fly by and we were soon saying our good bye's again at the 370 bus stop This routine went on for some weeks until one day I had some bad news my student friend was about to leave which meant I would have to pay his rent as up till now we had shared the cost of our room, this meant I could no longer stay there as I just would not be able to afford it. I went out in Romford looking for another place to stay this was very difficult and the only place I could find was a cheap scruffy place but begers cant be choosers so I reluctantly had to accept fate. Cynthia when she saw where I was living said you cant stay here She said I will have a word with my mother and see if you can live with us until things change for you I tried to talk her out of her suggestion but she would not take no for an answer it all happened so quick after that Informed my place of work that I would be leaving Cynthia told me to do this and I just seemed to do whatever she said So it wasn't long before I was sitting on the 370 alongside my Cynthia I couldn't believe how far we were going stop after stop we went past and it seemed like hours before she said we are here this is where we get off we then had to walk for about 200YDS up the avenue where Cynthia lived in (ward ave) the houses looked very grand as we arrived at No 88. Her mother greeted us very sternly Hmm she said so this is Alfred is it yes mum was Cynthia's reply as she closed the door we had just enterd by we are cold and hungry mum I know said her mother beconing me into the dining room she said sit there son we will soon have you fed your dinners are in the oven Cynthia get them out theres a dear and Cynthia and I where soon tucking in to a lovely stew her mother had made After that I was taken up stair's to what was to be my room it was a very small box room with a single bed that filled the room apart from a dining chair I only had a small suit case so it didn't take me long to unpack and I was soon coming down stairs again where I was usherd into the lounge Where there was a nice coal fire glowing red the room was nice and warm and felt very welcome to to me sitting on one side of the fire was Cynthia's mum and on the other side was an elderly gentleman he put his hand out for me to shake as his mother said this is my eldest son Leonard and I simply said Alfred as I sat myself down on the settee in front of the fire Cynthia was washing the dishes in the kitchen she finished the chores and came into the lounge and sat beside me on the settee. My new life seemed to start from here we started a wonderful courtship and all my horrorble past I think began to leave me, but it wasn't all good because on one of our evenings out in Grays I felt it was time to tell my Cynthia all about my children and my divorce and all the about the maintenance I was now paying which would be a big stumbling block in our future planning it was an awful shock to her but I just had to be honest with her if we were to have a future together and I did want that so much she must have loved me very much to come home from London and do all her chores and then travel all the way to Romford on that bus to see me this was true love and I truly loved her in return. After she got over the shock, she calmly said don't worry Darling together we will manage whatever it takes I said What will your mother say she wont like it Cynthia said but she will have to get over it In fact I will tell her to night When we get back home she was a very good diplomat and very strong in tackling problems well when we arrived back home it late as it was her plan to speak to her mother without her elder brother being there she said he would be in bed when we got home and she was right. Her mother was still up and where have you two been till now she asked Cynthia was in the kitchen putting the kettle on and from the kitchen she said Oh we saw a show and it didn't finish till late then in she came with the tea and we all settled back in our seats I have something to tell you mother don't tell me he's married is that it well Cynthia said sort of, well her mother said Cynthia said he was but is now divorced he has children also oh how many four I said and produced a photo of them for her to look at yes and they look well too who divorced who she added she divorced me but I am not sorry now I tried to reconcile with her Seven times and she just dint want to know I thought till death us do part meant something it did to me but not to her I suppose you will be kicking me out now I said. But her mother said I didn't say that and as long as you look after my girl I never will she added I haven't known you long but I think you are a nice boy then to Cynthia she said you know I will have to tell your brother Leonard about every thing but not the rest of the family thanks mum Cynthia said I do love him you know meaning me Well I soon found work with the local electricity board the South Eastern branch And While I had found work nearer home, Cynthia had done the same she no longer had to do that long journey to London each day and she was working in South Ockendon where I sometimes was working we would meet for lunch together at a pub and it was very good as time went on we were talking of getting married and Cynthia was going to be done out of a white wedding I was sad about this but my Cynthia didn't seem to mind so soon we were setting a date and place the date would be in September 10th and the place the Grays registry office So it was all planed and we where both very happy Cynthia's friends who took her to the dance hall where we first met they would be top of the list to attend then all of her large family and the brothers and their partners on my side just my Sister Ada and Harold her husband they travelled all the way from Liverpool on a motorbike and sidecar and I was very pleased to see them on my special day we had the reception in Cynthia's house and outside in her mothers lovely garden Where lots of photographs were taken Our honeymoon was to be in the seaside town of Eastbourne and two of Cynthia's friends saw us off on the train journey from G rays and they covered us in confetti to add to our embarrassment all the way to Eastbourne where we settled in to our boarding house and then went out for an evening stroll along the prom arm in arm very in love and then back to our boarding house and bed it a nice town to explore we noticed there was a local comedian plying his trade at a theatre his name "Denny Willis" it was on in the evening so we booked it and carried on with our exploring we found a nice restaurant and enjoyed our meal there we noticed a lot of pictures of "Denny Willis" on the wall and the waiter told us that the great man eats there so we just couldn't wait to get to the theatre to see this man well the show was very very good we just couldn't stop laughing After the show it was fish and chips time and we walked along the prom again eating them as we went an talking about the Show then back to our abode and bed the next day the sun was still shining it was a lovely sunny day again as we walked around the town we bought two small wooden elephants that Cynthia liked from an antique shop and soon we found ourselves at the restaurant with all the pictures on the wall and there in the corner was the great man himself the waiter said this couple are on their honeymoon to Mr Willis and he came over to the table to congratulate us we were chatting to him about the show when there was some noise coming from out side we looked out to see a bubble car had turned upside down by the curb so Denny and I rushed outside to turn it the right way up then we all be came good friends we had free tickets to his shows met some of his friends and my love for my Cynthia grew stronger day by day it was soon time to return to 88 ward ave and the real world again but as long as my new life partner was with me I felt very confident that I could now take all the bad knocks that this world could throw at me from now on. We were soon find out that the (cat had been let out of the bag) as reguards my four Children and my ex Cynthia's siblings soon let me know how they felt about this bad man being married to their baby sister not by words but by there silence so that when ever they came around to visit their mother I used to make myself scarce by going upstairs to our box room and burying myself in a magazine that I had delivered for that purpose in fact I used to smoke a lot in those days in the 1950's but after reading in my magazine "The New Scientist" on the damage I was doing to my lungs I never smoked again from that day. It was only at weekends and evenings That there was a problem because we both had to be at work a lot as I was short of money and we were both saving like mad to try and leave our box room and try to find something better it was very difficult to get council accommodation in those days you would register with the local council and wait in a queue it was a points system if you had ten children or if you were dying then you were allotted more points and you could jump to nearer the front of the housing queue. So all Cynthia and I could do was do plenty of over time and save like mad then the worst luck Cynthia was pregnant and we needed baby clothes and Things so we were spending as well as trying to save but we were very exited I couldn't wait to hold my own little baby again after being robed of my other children Cynthia had me attending night school to try to better myself and it was while I was at the thurock Technical collage That my dear Cynthia decided it was time for her to become a mum So getting the message I rushed home to find her outside in an ambulance as I approached the rear it drove off with me running behind it in a flood of tears but it went away from me to the hospital I went indoors to ask her brother to lend me his bicycle and off I went to the hospital and my dear Cynthia I was ushered into her Ward to see her bed at the end of the ward and a cot beside her bed the Flowers I had managed to buy on the way looked a bit sorry for themselves but the nurse took them away and brought back a lovely vase full I still think she must have added some Cynthia liked them as she told me it hadn't been nice for her and she made me promise there would be no more children as I was looking down at my son Paul he looked beautiful a good weight too 8.12 he was ours and we were looking forward to all the things we would do the three of us in the future I remember on a Sunday morning I would be dressed in my Sunday best and strolling off down Ward Ave proud as punch with our new baby son Paul in his new Pram I did this every Sunday While my Cynthia was doing her chores and then she would be getting the Sunday roast ready for the family we were still house hunting and saving as much as we could in the circumstances then one day my Cynthia said a girl friend of hers told her of an un furnished house to let, in Stanford le hope in a place called "Old Jenkins Close" It would be very expensive but my Cynthia said that we could just afford it if we tightend our belts even more and she was the one managing all our finances So decided to give it a go even though we didn't have any furniture Cynthia's friends said they would give us one dining room chair we had our bedding and a single bed and the baby's cot and pram And that was all but when our friends left and we shut our very own front door we felt so good there was a piece of card board laying on the floor and later in the day I went to the corner shop bought some crayons and drew and coloured picture and put it on our living room wall And Cynthia loved it and it wasn't even framed. Those were very happy days in our very own home I remember the man next door gave us some flowers in bloom to put in our front gardens and gradually our first house was looking more beautiful each day our baby Paul was growing older so we were soon able to put him in nursery we didn't have much choice but got on there very well and it enabled Cynthia to resume work as a secretary for the "Ford Motor Co" and we where soon getting back on our feet "As they say" As time went on I was soon able to buy a "Motor Bike" just a Honder 50 But it was better for my work and meant I could do more overtime because we were still having letters from my ex wife's solicitors saying she needed more money. So even though we were ok it was still very hard. Then to make matters worse on the 12th of January, my birthday I was getting read to go to work and Cynthia said don't go on the main road the A13 today not on your birthday so I promised her I would do as she asked and off I went on a lovely sunny day nice and dry roads along a quiet morning country road I wasn't going very fast I looked in my mirror to see a lorry behind me and then I woke to see Cynthia looking down at me where am I asked your in hospital dear she said you have had an accident I then realised I had bandage's and things all over me what about work Cynth I said I am at work the boss had me brought here when the police phoned and you don't have to worry I have told your firm. What time is it then she said its two o'clock you were laying in a ditch for two hours before anyone found you I am sorry dear don't be silly she said do you remember what happened I tried hard to remember but all I could remember was when I looked in my mirror and saw a lorry and I to this day can't remember anything else.

To this day I cannot remember anything about this accident. On my wife's next visit, she informed me that my employer's were not prepared to pay me for the day of the accident, but there was always my trade union to sort it out for me. And this assured her that everything was going to be alright so that calmed her that everything would be fine.

After a few weeks more the hospital discharged me, they told me to report at a convalescent home in "Clacton-on Sea". The home was on the outskirts of a village called "St Osyth". The home turned out to be a beautiful country house or mansion set in many acres of ground. I approached it via a "huge" gatehouse and at the far end of the drive ahead of me, there looking majestic in a September sunshine was the mansion.

That was to be my home for the next few weeks. I was greeted by a young nurse who took my small suitcase and ushered me to a small room off the main entrance hall where a more senior nurse welcomed me and bade me sit down while she examined the papers the hospital had given me to hand in here.

As I sat there looking around this what was a treatment room with its scales and glass cupboard's full of medicines the senior nurse or sister beconed me onto the scales. Then she took my pulse temperature and prepared to take my blood pressure. She started to read the rules to be obeyed while I was a patient here. She said first of all we want you to be happy while you are with us and we want you to eat as much of our lovely food that comes from our very own farm here on the estate. You must eat well even if you have two or more helpings we won't mind. The staff here are very **few in number. There are only two nurses and my self so we trust you to behave and enjoy your stay with us. Now nurse will show you to your room the room.**

The room the nurse took me to was wonderful with its oak panelled walls and chandelier lighting. I though I must be dreaming and only three beds in such a large room and what lovely beds. Having settled in I began to explore my new home. I found my way to a large hall where there was two guys playing snooker on a grand snooker table at the far end of the hall and some other guys sitting about reading or doing jigsaw puzzle's. There was one Chap though just looking out of one of the large windows. I spoke to him and asked him if I was dreaming he replied me to its good. Here isn't it then he began to tell me this was his second week and what he had found out about this wonderful place. It seems that the owner was a "Lord-de chair" who was "Winston Churchill's" righthand man who now spends a lot of his time abroad so he lets his beautiful mansion be used as a converlecent home for the very rich but in the later months of the year he lets the National Health use it for ordinary folk like me, one of the lucky ones. The estate was very large and very beautiful with all kinds of wild life roaming about like deer and there were lots of peackocks about. All arouind the home and the many different tress, it was all so lovely. Sometime the peacocks would look through my bedroom window perched on some large piece of ruin outside, and they certainly awakened us in the morning with their cry but we my room mates and I we didn't mind at all. We soon got used to it.

Visitors were allowed all t he time and my wife came to see me with our little son, Paul. I took her and our son out into the village for some creamed teas and a chat about everything my wife said that she had a very tiresome journey, and that our son had played her up all the way, which had been so bad to suffer all that embarrassment. I explained to her that I was fine, and that she need not come again as my stay in the home shouldn't be to long and that I would soon be home and enjoying each others company again. We had spent a nice time together and our son had fell asleep but it was soon time for her to depart so we made our way to the bus stop for her return bus the sun was going down I remember as we kissed goodbye. I stood for a while watching the bus disappear around a bend and then made my way back to my beautiful abode. The time went very quick and I soon found myself waiting for the same bus that I had seen my wife off a week or so ago. I was soon back in our lovely house again, and back to work. My wife was soon back working as a secretary with the "Ford Motor Co." having found a nursery school for our son. We began to enjoy life once again as before my accident we went places with our friends "Ted and Beryl" and we saw more of Cynthia's family.

Another interesting time was when my wife and I had been out shopping. We came back in our car a Ford Cortina and arrived at the back entrance to our house in Godman rd. And our little son Paul who had been playing with his friends in our neighbour's back garden came running to meet us, he was very excited as he told us he would be playing in a marching band this coming Saturday in "The Royal Albert hall, in London". This well we just thought it was something he had made up until that evening when we received a phone call from a "Mr. hall" asking if it was all right for Paul To go to the R.A.H. And he explained that he would be on the stage playing in the band. There would be a place for mum and dad on the coach and at the R.A.H. And of course a cost which we found very reasonable now it was Mum and dad who were excited and we couldn't wait for Saturday to come. The coach was very luxurious and we felt very proud of our son as we sat and enjoyed the sights of LONDON as we approached the ROYAL. ALBERT HALL in all its splendor. We that is all the mums and dads stood and applauded the young boys as they marched off the stage it made us so very proud of all the boys. Little did we know then what a joy it was to be part of this band as one journey followed another to all parts of Briton and then we were invited to take the Band to Europe. The first stop was to "LUDWIGSHAFEN AM RHEIN" in Germany. We my wife and I where to stay with a very lovely German family while our son stayed with another family close by. We were treated like Royalty by our lovely family they took us to many places of interest and beauty and this included "HEIDELBERG CASTLE" a place I had always wanted to visit.

The husband of the family on another occasion took me without my wife on a wine tasting run around the area. The idea was that Folk here did this to replenish their stock at home. It wasn't very long before I was more than merry I had never in my life tasted so many different wines in so short a time. When we got back after a lovely day out it was bed for me but I will never ever forget our lovely host's in Germany.

Our next Europian Trip was to "Chatellerault" A really lovely part of "FRANCE". My wife and I were fortunate to stay with a family who owned a "Bistro" a sort of pub and we were soon to be made to feel quite at home with an occasional brandy with our meals our host even tried to feed us snails we said no thanks until we realised it was all in fun and what we had in front of us at the dining table were "Olives". We enjoyed the fun of which there was lots from that first day onwards. The husband of our lovely family was also a jockey and we that is my dear wife and I were invited to travel to the race course which was on the other side of "Paris". On the day in question we were awakened at five am to get ready for our trip

We were driven in their beautiful Merc to a farm to collect our horse and trailer and as the sun was just about to appear we set off for our destination. The views as we travelled were wonderful. Eventually we arrived at the race course and met all the friends of our family who were busy getting a long line of tables together that is what the males of this very large group of friends were doing while the females were busy getting our breakfast ready. Then there was a lull in proceedings as the fact that it happened to be my dear wife Cynthia's birthday and all the males rushed to kiss her and wish her well and she was blushing quite red but joining in with all the merriment then we all sat down to breakfast. The food was plentiful and very tasty especially the hard boiled eggs I ate my fill and the we all worked to clear things away and get ready for the races of course my Cynthia and I had a flutter on our jockey. The races were the the ones were the jockey's sit behind the horse and the horse trots. It was our first time of seeing this type of horse racing but we enjoyed our day very much.

We were soon back in Chatellerault again and chatting together over drinks in our wonderful bistro. The next evening our host's took us out to a club and we drank and danced the night away with some more of their friends. Then it was to soon the day when we were to attend the last of our boys marching through Chatellerault with all the population out to applaud them for the displays they had done with the French boys marching bands in previous days since we arrived here. The mayor took the salute and it had all come to an end much to soon so we were soon on our way back to England.

Once settled back home it was work as usual for my Cynthia and I and back to school for our young son Paul. Then one day changed things for me. While working in a house as an Electrician I refused to connect a customers storage heater as I explained to the customer that I considered it dangerous but that was the worst thing because this consumer was a friend of my higher boss and I was put on suspension pending being sacked. I didn't know what to say to my dear Cynthia but there was always the trade union. So on the day of the inquisition as I chose to call it I stood outside this large office door for an eternity "not shivering I might say" before they called me in.

As I entered the room I observed a pocket size envelope being passed to my representative which soon disappeared into his jacket pocket. I had the feeling then that it wasn't going to be my day but in the end I was given a compromise which I don't think they expected me to take but to spite them I did. They offered me a job in the stores as "A storekeeper". I soon became very good at my job and was promoted to head keeper of our small stores with my wife still working I would give her all my wages and she would give me my pocket money each week. It was like that from that day and it has worked well. I have no regrets at this arrangement at all in fact I would go as far as to recommend it to other couples in similar circumstances it worked very well for us and we soon found ourselves back on our feet again

As time went by we eventually moved house the house we had at the time was our first and we loved it very much but we had the offer to buy and my Cynthia said yes. We could not afford to do this she held the purse strings so I went along with this adventure. Once the property was ours we went ahead with selling it and looking for pastures new we soon sold our lovely Godman Road house and found a beautiful very large house that had belonged to a very prominent family.

As we first entered our new abode there was a large picture of the house with the important family in attendance. The family were the famous "Bentall" family. Famous because the first Mr. Bentall had invented the plough and was so successful that he eventually made his own motor car a four cylinder. He would have gone far with this except I believe the dominance of the American car manufacturers the time so what he did do though was to open a large factory then needed workers brought them from far and wide built them homes.

And that was the birth of a new village Called "Heybridge" then opened large stores or perhaps his sons did in "Heybridge" Kingston on Thames" and Brighton" these I have shopped in there may be many more. He also built the house he lived in called the Towers made of solid concrete with ducts the first central heating in Great Britain. The house I was about to buy as the envy of Heybridge I am sure

We had grapevines both red and white and apple trees, and I loved it there, so my extra my extraordinary life rolled on. As we my wife and stood the other side to what was to be our new home in the village of, on the other side of the Colchester road we realised that we were never going to get across this road as the traffic was dense. We looked for the Road crossing but there was none to be seen.

Just then a lady with her two children joined us and said "Isn't this awful we have been on to the council for years to get us a road crossing but to know avail. Eventually the traffic eased enough for me to venture out into the road and stand there with my hand up "like a policeman" and helped the people across the road, a few more people had joined us. Anyway we got to our new house and there were some welcoming bright coloured balloons tied to the door knocker. We knew then that we were home all we had to do then was wait for the large removal van to arrive.

As days went by we blessed our good fortune at being in this lovely new house but this was all because of my dear wife and her stringent housekeeping. She even raided my pockets to find small change to bank something I do myself to this day. She had turned my turbulent life around and we began to make the most of the life we had there. We soon made lots of friends and neighbours, the one day while visit the local post office I met one of the members of the parish council. He also managed the post office and as he was serving me. asked why nothing had been done about a road crossing for our dangerous Colchester road. He informed me he had been trying for years to get something done about it.

So that was that but I promised myself that if there was ever a vacancy on the council that I would put myself forward as I was determined to get a road crossing. Well to my surprise while reading the local paper I found that there was a vacancy and that candidates for the position would be interviewed at the next parish meeting so my chance was here. I attended the meeting as a candidate interviewed and told that I would be informed one way or the other in the near future. Well then there was the watching for the postman time and then it came asked my wife to open the letter and she simple said you have got it. And gave me the letter to fully read and digest. Sure enough short of being sworn in at the next parish meeting I was now councillor Wynne.

It felt good but let me digress and return to the house we had in Godman Road Chadell Street Mary. While my new occupation was as a storekeeper I became very ill with chest infection was off work for quite a long time and the firm sent senior officials to my home to discuss the termination of my employment due to health. The reason was the result of the firms doctor's diagnosis which was "emphasyma" and I was discharged on a measly pension. The reason though it wasn't even discussed in those days was passive smoking because the people coming to the counter in my stores where always smoking as I served them, and I never smoked. In fact I wouldn't even sit with my colleagues as we sat for our breaks in the stores.

So now as a councillor, I was retired from my work of 30 odd years so could put all my effort into being a good Councillor would now commence my priority would be that road crossing that was so desperately needed by my constituents. But before that there was plenty to do as regards helping to deal with the various problems that would crop up from time to time. I wrote to and liaised with all the people who had the power to help with my crusade for my road crossing from M.P.S. TO PRIME MINISTER.

I was so determined and one day I received notice that the work would be starting on the road crossing. I was delighted and was congratulated for my work by my fellow councillators and all the local residents. My wife and I enjoyed our time in HEYBRIDGE. We became close friends of many nice people and the headmaster of the local school also. My son now had grown and had married and divorced and now had other liaisons and was even living in his own house quite a few miles away in VANGE NEAR BASILDON.

My wife and I hadn't had hardly any holidays since our honeymoon. We were out with a close friend of mine from my days at work PETER BROOKS and his wife JANNET who also lived in Heybridge just up the road. We stopped at a road side café and I saw my wife looking at some notices regarding things people wanted to see or buy etc but the card my wife was looking at was to do with a caravan holiday in North Wales. My wife was very interested in this so we took note of the PHONE NO and when we got back home she phoned about the holiday and came off the phone delighted turned to me and said can we go of course. I said I would have anywhere she wanted to go.

Well from then on it was all about this holiday. It was simple enough all I had to do was drive our loaded Sierra sapphire Ford car up four motorways the m25 m1 m6 and another to Shropshire but I didn't care my Cynthia was worth all of this and she was so excited about it all.

We made one stop in the m1 service station. We had a brief meal and then proceeded on our way. No sat nav in those days only a map on Cynthia's knee but we got to Shrewbry and then the A55 towards Caenarfon. Through there and on to the signpost saying FRON we took a very steep winding road to the very top and we were amongst the mountains of beautiful N/Wales. When the road finished we were at our holiday accommodation Beautiful Welsh cottage all on its own and a large caravan in the very large garden it looked very inviting and my Cynthia loved it and it got even nicer when we were greeted so warmly by the people who owned the cottage and the caravan. They introduced themselves as Mary and Sam and we were to leave everything and just relax on a wonder on the garden seat in front of the cottage. It was a lovely day Mary brought us a lovely tray of goodies and a welcome pot of tea which she began to pour into our cups. We sat and chatted while Sam took all our belongings into the lovely caravan. It was beautifully furnished inside.

As soon as we got sorted and Sam had told me how to operate the different things we were in what was to be our home for the next two weeks. So began our four years of travelling to N/Wales every time my wife's holidays came around off we would go to our caravan and Sam and Mary my wife loved Wales and the beautiful mountains.

I did take her up to the top of Snowdon on the train and then one day we were sitting outside our caravan just being lazy sunning ourselves when Sam came to us and said so you think you have seen all of Wales well he said you haven't seen the big mansion house just 5 minutes away from here and its open to the public. It is called

"Clynllifon" and it used to belong to the "Wynne" family. I said your Kidding me Sam. No he said it is true. Cynthia said well dear it would be nice so we dressed and back into Bettsy our faithful car. We were soon looking at this beautiful mansion house it was like something out of a film and the grounds where magnificent to walk on with all different trees and flowering shrubs everywhere. We looked then on entering the grand hall

At the entrance to the house there on the wall was the history of the Wynne family who as Sam had said once owned this magnificent mansion house I read and took in all I could about the history of the Wynne family of Glynllifon and wondered could I be related to this family. Well with my head in the clouds I drove back to the caravan and Sam who jokingly said well sir do I have to bow we laughed it off for the rest of the night. But I said to Cynthia they owned property all over N/Wales it says here, I was still reading the history the next morning. I then said we could make a sort of pilgrimage to all their property's. We could enjoy all the scenic view as we travelled along but its up to you dear I meant it because I realised that I was becoming obsessed with the Glynllifon Wynnes I wonder why.

Well the first place we went was in "LLANRWST". It was the home of Sir John Wynne in the 16th cent. It was called "Gwydir Castle" This was more of a grand house than a castle, but it had like a lot of the Wynne grand houses lots of interesting history. There are many of these large houses in N/Wales Like "Bodfan" Wynstay" "Harden Castle, and the grand house of Sir Robert Wynne in Conway and history like the fact that' Gladstone the famous PRIME MINISTER was married to a Glynllifon Wynne and that Charles the first spent some time with his queen at "Gwydir Castle" and Later George V. spent time there with Mary before he was king and later still the present Prince of Wales Charles has also spent time there

I cannot ever understand the Council of Gwynedd why the haven't realised the tourist benefit on their doorstep. If only they opened their eye's even the "USSR" are making millions by not destroying places like the "Winter Palace" yet the Gwynedd council cannot get rid of the history of this Wynne family quick enough. "Strange".

Well my wife Cynthia and I certainly loved Wales and so much so that instead of travelling all the way from Essex every year we asked our son Paul if he would mind if we moved to N/Wales bearing in mind he was settled now and fully grown and living in his own house. His remark go for it Dad. He seemed to not mind at all so we My wife Cynthia and I Who had also retired from working at the "Ford Motor Co" started to make plans to move to the Caernarfon area of Gwynedd N/Wales. But first we must sell our lovely house and we soon had offers but not enough.

As we were getting offers we realised that we must find a house in N/Wales quickly in case we had an offer we couldn't refuse. So we were travelling back and forth up those four motor ways but this time at some times at 90o mph there and back in a day.

After we had viewed a few houses this went on for quite a few weeks and we still hadn't decided on our future home and worse we hadn't had that offer that we would except yet. But we didn't give up hope.

And one day it came that all important offer that we had asked for in the first place and the people wanted to move in as quick as possible. So we found ourselves homeless in the middle of "betws-y-coed and there was an information beauro still open as we needed somewhere to stay that night. The staff phoned around the Caearnarfon area and found us a bed and breakfast place so that was fine. The next day we went to an estate agent who gave us a sheaf of papers of places to view. The first one we looked at my wife said this is exactly what we want and that was that. Then it was back to Essex and finish the packing and wait for that phone call to say it was all done that soon came we signed the necessary docs.

Then back home to wait for two pantechnicon's to arrive load up and we left before them and went along those four motorways for the last time. Our new house was there in the moonlight but no vans in sight but the lady next door Delyth came out of her house with a nice welcome cup of tea and bade us welcome as a new neighbour.

About two hours later one of the pantechnicon vans turned up and started to unload all our stuff into the house and the garage. It was nearly empty when the other one arrived and all the rest of the of the stuff we had to put in the Garage. The garage was so full we had trouble shutting the door the reason for this in our haste to finalise the move we over looked the fact that the new house in N/Wales was a lot smaller than the one in Essex so we had brought too much stuff with us to our new house. While I had been busy with the removal men Cynthia had been making a bed for us so I thanked the men generously waved them off and returned to my dear wife who had just finished making a new pot of tea. And as we sat down just the two of us we breathed a sigh of relief and went to our bed. This was the dawn of the new "millennium" and everything was going to be wonderful, this is how we were feeling at the time. We worked morning and night then off and on for quite a few weeks to get our new house in order, my wife busy with curtains and such and I with placing of carpets and furniture and our new home began to feel like home.

Of course we did get out in our car for a change of scenery and weekly shopping, so our work got less each day and we began to enjoy this new country of Wales we planned a holiday to Cardigan somewhere we hadn't been before we found in the "British legion" mag someone letting a cottage for two weeks. We decided that is just the holiday we would have, so we started crossing off the days. Then one day we found ourselves in our Seiera saphire heading towards Cardigan. We arrived in good time and was greeted by the owner a very nice lady who gave us a tour of the cottage and made us very welcome it was quite lovely and we soon settled in our new abode and got used to things we had to do like putting out the milk bottles each night for the milkman. A nice breakfast and then to explore the town it was all that we expected it to be a lovely holiday town. Then we had to find a beach but there didn't seem to be one then on asking a local bar tender he put us in the right direction for one of the loveliest beaches I have ever seen and not a lot of people on it. We got our chairs and a table out of the car together with our picnic basket.

My Cynthia would sit on her chair reading or knitting or cross stitching while I would be swimming not to far away so I could return the occasional wave from her. We Travelled around the area and also took in the botanical gardens and St. David's Cathedral also the library at Aberystwyth. We enjoyed ourselves so much we decided to stay for a further week. Then it was back to our lovely house in Bontnewydd 2 miles form Caernarfon the next episode to our new life was my wife's conservatory that's what my dear Cynthia wanted so that is what she would have. But where would it go there wasn't a wall it could go against but I came up with a solution the garage at the side of the house, if I used the same base and dimensions it would go there and the planning permission couldn't be refused and she soon had her wish my Cynthia had her conservatory. I had bought some land adjoining our property so I had GARAGE Built on there so the next thing to enhance our new house was to have the walls pebble dashed and the result was stunning. The house looked lovely now and my Cynthia was very pleased the garden was soon looking beautiful so this was it we had arrived. We started to have visitors even Cynthia's family members from Canada while they were staying in the U.K. came to see us and Cynthia's nieces and nephew came. They were good times then this was what we both wanted in our retirement.

We were looking forward to many more years of this but in 2003 it all changed for the worst my Cynthia started to accuse me of seeing other women. I had no idea of what she was talking about when she said that she had seen them in the garden. I tried to assure her that what she was thinking was not true but it was all in vein while attending our doctor I asked him about my dear wife's behaviour and he said it sounds like a mental problem to me and just to keep an eye on her. I began to think about other things that seemed strange that she did in the past like in our other house in Essex my Daughter knocked at our door one day my wife opened the door to her but asked me who it was. That was strange then there were the times we went out shopping and she would turn the wrong way coming out of a shop that was strange also I thought. Then she went shopping on her own on the bus one day from where we lived now and my neighbour found her walking back along the main road and stopped his car and drove her home she had taken the wrong bus but it wasn't like her and that was the start of what was to become like a nightmare to me. She was diagnosed with dementure and they put her on warfrin tablets that I had to manage the strict dosage of that was when she began to not notice me and gradually she didn't know who I was and she couldn't do her knitting or writing and dressing herself. She would just sit in her chair with a blank look on her face. I had lost my dear Cynthia but I could cuddle her whenever I liked so that was nice but where had my Cynthia gone. I suddenly felt quite alone. As I remember some of the good times since we moved to N/Wales I recall the time Cynthia said as we are not far from Ireland perhaps we could go sometime so we looked up how we could go there and found there was a coach trip starting from not to far from where we lived. The itinery said we would be catching the ferry from Holyhead to Dun laoghaire, we soon found ourselves on the fast ferry and loving every minute a very smooth crossing found us with time to spare the coach driver told us so as a bonus he would take us around Dublin and it was a lovely day and the whole coach were singing as we made our way out of Dublin and toward our hotel that was in Killarney and what a beautiful place we where in that was a lovely holiday to recall.

Well as I said things went very bad for us it 2003. While sitting on our settee one day watching the television together I felt that "TO PUT IT RUDELY" I had passed wind but to my horror it was thick very dark red blood and it wouldn't stop and with my wife in her state all I could think about was her but I was quickly on the phone to my doctor but could only speak to a nurse. I told her the state I was in with all this blood. I could only presume that it must be a blood vessel that had burst so there was no way of stopping it at all

The nurse said she would get on to the doctor right away then she quickly phoned me back to say the doctor was on his way but had ordered an ambulance for me and then there was a knock at the door and it was the ambulance. The doctor also the nurse I was worried about my Cynthia they said she will be coming too she was all confused and did not know what was happening to me. I felt so sorry for her we were alone with no one except the ambulance crew. I had the presence of mind to turn everything off and lock the doors. but I was still bleeding very bad blood everywhere. When I got myself in the ambulance with my dear frightened Cynthia I tried to comfort her as best I could in the ambulance. I asked the attendant if he could give me some paper to mop up the blood still pouring out of my backside so he gave me a big roll off blue paper that I started to stuff down my trousers. We arrived at the hospital I was put on a trolley and whisked away to a ward where the nurses were sitting chatting to each other they said to the ambulance men sit him on the bed in ward something we will attend to him in a minute still losing blood and feeling weaker by the minute I found a toilet I sat down on the toilet and felt the last drop of blood leave me.

I woke sometime later in a bed lose to where the nurses were chatting when I came in. I shouted my wife's name and was told to be quiet they said I was lucky to still be alive it was the crash team that had saved me after Maltese boy had found me on the floor in the toilet but where was my wife my Cynthia we haven't seen anyone was the nurses reply she must be somewhere. I told them of her condition and they said they would find her if she is in the hospital. I was frantic with worry as they told me she wasn't in the hospital and that they had notified the police then. Sometime later they said they had found her one of my neighbour, visiting had found her and took her to their home so she was safe I fell into a deep sleep.